The Trouble With Big Data

Bloomsbury Studies in Digital Cultures

Series Editors
Anthony Mandal and Jenny Kidd

This series responds to a rapidly changing digital world, one which permeates both our everyday lives and the broader philosophical challenges that accrue in its wake. It is inter- and trans-disciplinary, situated at the meeting points of the digital humanities, digital media and cultural studies, and research into digital ethics.

While the series will tackle the 'digital humanities' in its broadest sense, its ambition is to broaden focus beyond areas typically associated with the digital humanities to encompass a range of approaches to the digital, whether these be digital humanities, digital media studies or digital arts practice.

Titles in the series
Queer Data, Kevin Guyan

Forthcoming titles
Human Exploits, Cyberpunk and the Digital Humanities, Aaron Mauro
Ambient Stories in Practice and Research, Edited by Amy Spencer
Metamodernism and the Postdigital in the Contemporary Novel, Spencer Jordan

The Trouble With Big Data

*How Datafication Displaces
Cultural Practices*

Jennifer Edmond, Nicola Horsley,
Jörg Lehmann and Mike Priddy

BLOOMSBURY ACADEMIC
LONDON • NEW YORK • OXFORD • NEW DELHI • SYDNEY

BLOOMSBURY ACADEMIC
Bloomsbury Publishing Plc
50 Bedford Square, London, WC1B 3DP, UK
1385 Broadway, New York, NY 10018, USA
29 Earlsfort Terrace, Dublin 2, Ireland

BLOOMSBURY, BLOOMSBURY ACADEMIC and the Diana logo are
trademarks of Bloomsbury Publishing Plc

First published in Great Britain 2022
This paperback edition published 2023

Series design by Rebecca Heselton
Cover image © Christoph Burgstedt / Alamy Stock Photo

A catalogue record for this book is available from the British Library.

A catalog record for this book is available from the Library of Congress.

ISBN: HB: 978-1-3502-3962-3
        PB: 978-1-3502-3966-1
        ePDF: 978-1-3502-3963-0
        eBook: 978-1-3502-3964-7

Series: Bloomsbury Studies in Digital Cultures

Typeset by Integra Software Services Pvt. Ltd.

This book is available as open access through the Bloomsbury Open programme and is available on www.bloomsburycollections.com. It is funded by Trinity College Dublin, DARIAH-EU and the European Commission.

Contents

Acknowledgements

We would like to thank all of the contributors to the KPLEX project, in particular the interviewees, who gave so generously of their time, and our colleagues on the project team: Deirdre Byrne, Michelle Doran, Elisabeth Huber, Rihards Kalnins, Georgina Nugent Folan, Thomas Stodulka and Cydney Thompson.

Finally, we are grateful to the European Commission for funding the original Knowledge Complexity Project, under Grant Agreement 732340.

Viewing big data through the lens of culture

The development of this book began, as so many good stories do, with a group of people locked in a conflict. What made this conflict all the more intense was the fact that everyone in the room agreed what needed to be done, and yet none of them was satisfied with the outcome of previous attempts to meet the agreed requirement. They needed to share data.

The people in question were an interdisciplinary group of researchers, including historians, computer scientists and collections experts, trying to build an innovative platform to support historical research. This aspect of the project had largely stalled, due to what we ultimately recognized as a malfunction in communication. In essence, each party was working from a completely different definition of the word data, and a different understanding of what was possible and available as data to drive and populate the system.

In fairness, this problem actually began well outside of the group that had gathered, as the agency that had funded the project had done so already under something of a misconception about historical data, namely that historical resources were largely already available in digital forms, and merely needed to be somehow aggregated to facilitate their use. The historians in the group were of course deeply suspicious of this: they were keenly aware that only a fragment of the resources they needed were digitized, and greatly unevenly at that. They also weren't really confident about the word data, as it wouldn't be the word they would normally apply to their sources. But they took the impression from their technical colleagues that this word was somehow coterminous with 'inputs' and therefore began to offer small, rich, heterogeneous or indeed analog collections as examples. What the technical development team needed and wanted, however, was something more akin to 'big data': relatively homogeneous, relatively well-prepared, machine-readable full text able to support investigation of complex research questions. The collections experts from cultural heritage institutions, however, knew that realistically what was available and processable was not the research data itself, but rather the finding aids and collections metadata.

In retrospect, it is easy to see how these three different communities and perspectives would bring completely different conceptualizations of the word data to this collaboration, but at the time, this source of disconnection proved hugely challenging to tease out and manage. This left some members of the project team to wonder: if this smart, but diverse, group could end up so stymied by the gaps between their differing understandings of what the word data might encompass, was it possible that this same issue played out in other projects, sectors and arenas of life as well?

The KPLEX project

A second project was devised to test this hypothesis, and its findings form the core of the evidence presented in this book. This project, called 'Knowledge Complexity' (or KPLEX for short) was constructed to seek out these kinds of gaps and biases in research based on big data, harnessing in particular a multidisciplinary, but culturally centred, approach to this challenge. Specifically, the KPLEX project was moulded around three potential sources of miscommunication within teams undertaking data-related research, gaps that could also be found disrupting progress for research projects, as well as for the individual and industrial users some of this work was ultimately destined to serve. This phenomenon, whether unnoticed, convenient or intentional, resulted in what one of the authors of this book referred to as a game being played of mutual misunderstanding, according to which all sides may feel they have won, but only because they are using different rule books.

To approach this subtle and deeply engrained challenge, we defined three strands to our approach: In the first of these, we determined to look at issues of language and discourse around data, the heterogeneity of definitions of data, and the implications of this state of multiple, faceted common understandings. In particular, we also looked at the perceived tensions between data and narrative, as the building blocks of two different sensemaking techniques (one on the ascendant, one seemingly as old as our species), and the contrasts in these processes in their management of the iterative and nonlinear aspects of knowledge creation. We hoped that in this way we would be able to capture not just what the computational approach to knowledge creation might flatten, but also the concomitant processes developed not necessarily by humanists, but by humans, to preserve and make meaning from these noisy signals.

Within this strand, we particularly leveraged methods and perspectives from literary studies and historical research. For example, provenance is a key concept for historians and collections management professionals: indeed, a piece of evidence loses its authority utterly if its provenance is not clear. But in big data systems, provenance data is more likely to be looked upon as noise than signal. This is an understandable response to the problem of complexity and volume, even in the realm of cultural data: indeed, as a recent newspaper article puts it, 'the digitization of cultural heritage is booming, but it happens to be messy and chaotic. Scientists therefore cannot find or search through numerous sources'.[1] Cultural signals are ambiguous, polysemic, often conflicting and contradictory. This is true even in the 'low context' cultures (see the discussion of this characteristic in Chapter 8), where a greater cultural permeability is facilitated by explicitness in the communication and day-to-day deployment of cultural norms and practices. This is inscribed most visibly in language, but also in personal interactions, in religious practices, and in artistic production. In order to transform culture into data, its elements – as all phenomena that are being rendered as data – have to be classified, divided and filed into taxonomies and ontologies. This process of 'data-fication' thereby robs them of their polysemy, or at least reduces it.

The question remains open, however, of what the scientists referenced above would do with data they might find in a simplified system, once they found it, however, as the simplification that comes with greater aggregation and interrogability is also an impoverishment in terms of depth and complexity. Digging into these differences, the manner in which provenance is preserved in some systems, the nature of what provenance means for research: all of this is yet to be described and expressed in a manner that can assist developers to better enable similar transparency and flexibility in data-driven research to what historians and related disciplinary communities have developed over time.

It is difficult to speak of historical research only through the lens of the historian, however, as the interdependency between cultural research and the cultural heritage institution is a long-standing and productive one. For this reason, the KPLEX project also looked at the production of catalogue metadata for objects: as holdovers from a pre-digital age of physical catalogues, as the most common data to be found in digital systems of cultural data, as structured data of a sort that is easy to aggregate, as a draw on cultural institution resources that must create it in their digital systems, and as marks of human interpretation and occasional error. In the words of Johanna Drucker: 'Arguably, few other textual forms will have greater impact on the way we read, receive, search, access, use, and engage with the primary materials of humanities studies than the metadata structures that organize and present that knowledge in digital form.[2]

You cannot look at these established practices in the context of big data, however, without also looking into how emerging computational and information retrieval approaches, such as ultra-large systems and deep learning, but also things as mundane as keyword search, may be displacing the production of such metadata, removing the human investment and replacing it with a proxy that may or may not serve quite the same function. It was this trend towards knowledge loss that formed our second strand of investigation. According to the 2017 ENUMERATE Core 4 survey, only 22 per cent of the analog collections of European heritage institutions had at that time been digitized.[3] The survey reached only a limited number of respondents: less than 1,000 institutions over twenty-eight countries (including respondents from countries outside Europe, which were excluded from the analysis), which surely capture the major national institutions but not local or specialized ones.[4] Although the ENUMERATE report does not break down these results by country, one has to imagine that there would be large differences in the availability of data from some countries over others. Because so much of this data has not been digitized, it remains 'hidden' from potential users. This may have always been the case, as there have always been inaccessible collections, but in a digital world, the stakes and the perceptions are changing. The fact that so much other material is available online, and that an increasing proportion of the most well-used and well-financed cultural collections are as well, means that the reasonable assumption of the non-expert user of these collections is that what cannot be found does not exist (whereas in the analog age, collections would be physically contextualized with their complements, leaving the more likely assumption to be that more information existed, but could not be accessed). The threat that our narratives of histories and national identities might thin out to become based on only the most visible sources, places and narratives is high.

Data is not only hidden from the aggregated, on-line view because it has not been digitized, however. Increasingly, users are becoming frustrated with digital silos. The current paradigm is not that one visits a number of news or information sites, but that one channels one's content through an intermediary, such as Facebook or Twitter. The increase in the use of syndicated feeds such as RSS (Really Simple Syndication), or data access modalities that go around the human-readable interfaces such as APIs (Application Programming Interfaces), among many other technologies (including personalization and adaptation algorithms), evidences this preference. Cultural heritage institutions (CHIs) have adapted to this paradigm shift by establishing their own curated spaces within these channels, but in spite of this 'pushing out' response, the vast majority of their data cannot yet be 'pulled in' by developers wanting to feature cultural content. The biggest exception to this rule in Europe is Europeana, which has a very popular API and makes the metadata it delivers available under an open CC-0 reuse licence.[5] Most national, regional or local institutions hesitate to do the same, however, in part because of technical barriers, but also to a great extent because they do not trust the intermediaries and re-use paradigms that are emerging. They also may themselves not be in possession of full knowledge regarding the nature and import of what they hold, as the traditional symbiosis between the users of collections (i.e. the historians and other researchers) was based upon a division of knowledge, which has never been systematically integrated back into the CHIs. These institutions have developed over centuries to protect the provenance of items in their care, and to prevent their destruction or abuse. Not enough is known about how the digital age impacts upon this mission, and whether the hesitation to release data into shared platforms is merely risk-aversion, or whether this can tell us something critical about our current conceptions of data, and our current data-sharing environment.

This investigation was underpinned by the concept of the sharing of cultural data as a part of the institutions' 'public task'. This is a key concept, as it defines not just the generic mission of the institution, but also their responsibilities under the Public Service Information Directive to make the information they hold open.[6] The 2012 discussion of the position of the CHIs under this directive began to define some of the parameters for what KPLEX would investigate: the fact that CHIs often don't 'own' their own content in a clear way, the heterogeneity of descriptions across types of institutions and collections, the conflict between business models privileging digital access and the wider concepts of public good, among others.

Finally, the KPLEX project's third area of focus was to take a comparative approach to a range of research processes, humanities and cultural studies among them, in order to understand the range of strategies professional researchers were deploying in the integration of data into their knowledge creation processes. In February 2016, the European Commission released a list of actions under the heading of a 'Draft Open Science Agenda'.[7] Many of the actions listed there, such as increasing the reliability, efficiency and responsiveness of scientific enquiry, would be wholeheartedly supported by humanists and social scientists as well as by physical or natural scientists. But the nature of humanities data is such that even within the digital humanities, where research processes are better optimized towards the sharing of digital data, sharing of 'raw data' remains the exception rather than the norm.

There are a number of reasons for this. First of all, in many cases, ownership of the underlying input data used by humanists is unclear, and therefore the question of what can be shared or reused is one which the individual researcher cannot independently answer (this issue will be dealt with in the context of the topic described above). There are deeper issues, however, based in the nature of the epistemic processes of the humanities that act as further barriers to reuse of humanities data. Very little research exists in this topic to date, although barriers to reuse of digital humanities projects do provide an interesting baseline for starting an investigation. For example, the LAIRAH project pointed towards a number of key issues leading to a lack of reuse of digital data prepared by research projects.[8] In particular, the lack of an early conceptualization of who the future user of the data might be and how they might use it was a key deterrent to future use. While this lack may be seen as a weakness from a reuse standpoint, it is likely that the organization of data or the curation of resources chosen in such projects was driven by the research questions in the mind of the original researcher, and that this organizational model was key to their epistemic process. As the results of research into humanistic research processes[9] have demonstrated, the 'instrumentation' of the humanities researcher consists of a dense web of primary, secondary and methodological or theoretical inputs, which the researcher traverses and recombines to create knowledge. This synthetic approach makes the nature of the data, even at its 'raw' stage, somewhat hybrid, and already marked by the curatorial impulse that is preparing it to contribute to insight.

This aspect may be more pronounced in the humanities than in other fields, but the individual element is present in any human-triggered process leading to the production or gathering of data. Another element of this is the emotional. Emotions are motivators for action and interaction that relate to social, cultural, economic and physiological needs and wants. Emotions are crucial factors in relating or disconnecting people from each other. They help researchers to experientially assess their environments, but this aspect of the research process is considered taboo, as noise that obscures the true 'factual signal', and as less 'scientific' (seen in terms of strictly Western colonialist paradigms of knowledge creation[10]) than other possible contributors to scientific observation and analysis. What we need is more conceptual clarity when we assess global knowledge and translate it into federated, shared digital datasets. We used this frame of reference, that of emotion researchers, to explore the data creation processes of the humanities and related research fields to understand how they combine pools of information and other forms of intellectual processing to create data that resists datafication and 'like-with-like' federation with similar results. In particular, we were interested in locating 'failure points' in data, that is, points at which data becomes unusable, what characterizes these points and what a researcher does about it.

In sum, while we did not set out to position KPLEX as a digital humanities project, ultimately we seem to have done so, harnessing the emerging perspectives of critical digital humanities approaches[11] to turn eyes attuned to both cultural and humanistic forces at play as well as the impact of engineered knowledge technologies towards objects of study outside of the humanities themselves. Though we drew from the work and methods of social science, information science and computer science, our core desire from the outset was to look at the cultures, languages, values and beliefs at play below the surface of big data research, and this also comprises what we see as the primary contribution of the project.

The KPLEX interviews

The team that investigated these issues within the KPLEX project harnessed a number of methods, including an extensive engagement with secondary research across a number of fields, surveys, data-mining exercises, participation in relevant meetings and presentations and so on. Of particular importance, however, was the production of a corpus of interviews, thirty-eight in total, each of approximately one hour in length. The subjects of these interviews were roughly evenly split between participants representing three perspectives: computer scientists working with cultural data, interdisciplinary researchers, all focused on human emotion but with different home disciplines and levels of data intensity in their approaches, and cultural heritage professionals charged with preserving and making cultural source data accessible. In each cohort, the selected participants' work had a cultural element but was conceived of in terms of other disciplines (computer science, neuroscience, computational linguistics, etc.), or, in the case of the cultural heritage professionals, crossed boundaries between a number of disciplines. Although every group was interviewed with the intention of exploring their attitudes and practices towards and within big data research environments, the interview protocols used were tailored in each case to the professional discourse and specific concerns of that cohort, as well as to the facet of the project's research questions their input was most likely to shed light on.

Anonymized transcripts of these interviews are openly available as research data and they will be cited extensively in the course of this book.[12] It is an understatement to say that they provide a valuable and unique perspective on some of the darker sides of data-driven research, its propensity to incorporate biases of the teams and processes that assemble and use it, the risks it poses to individuals and cultural codes and the manner in which it tends to obscure other forms of sensemaking, when we in fact need more, not fewer, ways of approaching complex problems.

These results were collected, analysed and filtered through the perspectives of the full KPLEX team, which included researchers steeped in the practices of literary studies, history, anthropology, sociology, information science, software development and the digital humanities. As such, this team was able to bring a fresh perspective to existing work emerging from science and technology studies, looking at not only how big data research and development practices shape our economy and society, but how it becomes entangled with fundamental aspects of our culture: how we talk, what we accept and rebel against, whom we believe, how we come to understand the world and our place in it, who we think we are (and who we think others might be), the evidence we base these identities and cultural memories on, how we build hierarchies and social capital and so forth. We were able to apply this view from another perspective, and indeed to use our position and those of many of our interview subjects, as professionally trained seekers of knowledge, to explore these specialized processes, and the manner in which biases, quirks and flaws in them seemed to trickle down into wider social and cultural challenges.

Knowledge complexity 'in the wild'

The generation, gathering, analysis and interpretation of data have been central to knowledge creation and claims to truth since the first academic disciplines began to emerge. Research that makes use of data that can be seen to 'speak for themselves' has been known to leave a lasting mark on our culture; such is their capacity for capturing the popular imagination. Just as the Covid-19 pandemic has focused minds on a singular goal, eclipsing other priorities, widespread outbreaks of cholera in the 1800s led to concerted efforts in tracking the spread of disease, including John Snow's contamination analysis and pioneering maps – an early example of accessible data visualization that crossed into the social sciences with Charles Booth's colour coding of neighbourhoods by social class. In spite of the underlying data-centrism of Booth's iconic visualization, however, it is important to note that this was as much an investigation of culture as of social or indeed epidemiological evidence about communities, habits and trust as well as about bacteria and poverty.

Such iconic representations of data have come to stand for the progress made by our most celebrated innovators across the academic spectrum. Recent digitization initiatives have sought to expand the potential of facilitating the uptake of data-driven methods for areas of study previously seen as necessarily resistant. Arts, humanities and social science methods in particular were seen as intrinsically concerned with issues the digital did not easily encompass, such as close examination of the provenance and unique qualities of sources, considering them in their original contexts, looking for rich exemplars rather than large statistical patterns, slow processes and the fundamentally analog. This digital turn is part of a general trend whereby the research community and society at large have come to view data themselves as offering the answers – and even the questions – that bring us closer to understanding ourselves than the conventional methods of the humanities and social sciences. The reputation of the scientific method as a gold standard and perceptions of the essential 'purity' of data themselves seem invulnerable to even high-profile scandals. Whether duped by the publication of a counterfeit data-linking exercise in *The Lancet*[13] or the havoc wreaked by a 'mutant algorithm' deciding the grades by which young people's admission to university would be decided,[14] the tendency is to decry a wasted opportunity to properly harness the revealing powers of the data as always more objective than a fallible human counterpart decision-making process (in spite of the similar levels of bias and inappropriate modelling possible in each paradigm).

And so data have come to be seen as 'reusable goods',[15] their value no longer subject to interpretation by specialists in a particular discipline but dependent on their malleability to serve new, unpredicted purposes as they are aggregated with other data plucked from disparate contexts. This divergence from knowledge norms exemplified by Bernstein's *bounded knowledge code*[16] disrupts the process of knowledge creation and discovery, recalibrating its fundamental dynamics away from archival classification values that have been optimized for the needs of professional historical researchers, through a shift in practices located in institutional, governmental and commercial spheres. The standardization of data that began with trade between food markets accelerated with epidemics and facilitated globalization. It was put to use in building global infrastructures for sharing digitized data from most scientific disciplines from the 1970s, expanding through the ubiquity of personal computers and faster processing systems to our current demand for instant query fulfilment. Big data's hegemonic position has been cemented by the favour it has found in funding priorities and the policies and practices they have reinforced and engendered.

Sceptics of this hegemony, such as Donna Haraway, have instead advocated 'situated knowledges'. 'Situated knowledges are about communities, not about isolated individuals.' Haraway commented that '(i)mmortality and omnipotence are not our goals', nor is the splitting of subject and object.

> But we could use some enforceable, reliable accounts of things not reducible to power moves and agonistic, high-status games of rhetoric or to scientistic, positivist arrogance. This point applies whether we are talking about genes, social classes, elementary particles, genders, races, or texts; the point applies to the exact, natural, social, and human sciences, despite the slippery ambiguities of the words 'objectivity' and 'science' as we slide around the discursive terrain.[17]

And yet, the manner in which data are collected, used, reused, conceptualized and enshrined in language seems almost to demand and insist upon occupying a status above situatedness, a contextless state in line with the omniscience and omnipotence to which they seem to be granted a claim. (W. Edwards Deming was famously credited with coining the phrase: 'In God we trust. All others, bring data.') But we are our data, it is created not given, and therefore it is, for all the veneer of objectivity its champions want to place upon it, as fallible as we are and bound to human ideation, hierarchies, values and imaginaries – in other words to our culture. This obstacle, and the frustration that resulted in trying to work within its shadow as researchers that had to regularly transverse the boundaries between data-driven exploration and the qualitative traditions of cultural studies to pursue their objects of study, was the inspiration for this book.

As we shall see in Chapter 2's consideration of the linguistic images used to represent the idea of data, there is a disconnect between the enthusiasm for data as a panacea and the struggle of the popular imagination to visualize data as a concept. Metaphors play a similar role in our sensemaking practices, and the metaphors we use to understand data are of critical importance as, according to Star, 'power is about *whose* metaphor brings worlds together, and holds them there'[18] and power in its many forms is a concern we will come to in Chapter 7. Euphemisms used by big tech companies to describe what they are then show what a slippery terrain we're on: so how do we get a grip on these fundamental tenets of our era? Models like the Data Information Knowledge Wisdom (DIKW) hierarchy over-simplify data use by positioning data as a foundation from which we steadily build towards the keystone of wisdom. Leonelli instead advocates a relational approach to data and knowledge claims,[19] which adopts a reflexivity that, in practice, acknowledges the roles of creators of data and knowledge and their 'response-ability'[20] and requires a depth of engagement in the process that is not reflected in the norms of ethical guidelines. Leonelli also sees ethical box-ticking exercises as part of a system that upholds a simplistic view of data processing that denies context and the involvement of humans.[21]

As we shall see on our journey through the dimensions of data, knowledge and truth (and especially in Chapters 3 and 4), data practices have emerged through different traditions experiencing different digital disruptions. Ribes and Jackson's investigation of the workings of the data archive describes how 'the work of sustaining massive repositories reveals only a thin slice in the long chain of coordinated action that stretches back directly to a multitude of local sites and operations through which data in their "raw" form get mined, minted and produced'.[22] What remain at repositories are the distilled products of these field sites; behind these centres lie an even more occluded set of activities that produce those data themselves. Extant research has not fully documented the tensions of the application of the 'principles of information hiding'[23] to traditional archival practices, nor the extent to which existing metadata and practices across the sector already represent a big data approach to historical and cultural sources. *Archival thinking* and the organization of knowledge represent distinct cultures with their own values and norms while always anticipating change. Over seventy years ago, Broadfield described how knowledge classification systems cannot last forever and called for declines in technology to be properly managed to preserve knowledge, arguing that '[all] classifications in their existing forms are destined to become dust; sensitive adjustment should enable the classifier to consign them to dust himself [sic], instead of allowing the common enemy Time to do so'.[24] More recently, research has suggested that archivists are constantly changing and adapting their practices and systems up to and into the big data era.[25]

Accordingly, the story of the organization of knowledge takes us into the development of 'scientific' practices synonymous with professionalization (and, as Susskind and Susskind have shown, that tee up the replacement of professions with machines[26]), the growth of computer use from basic sorting functions to routine work to transforming practice, and the shift in decision making from the traditional gatekeepers of knowledge to data specialists testing the reach of technologies developed for other purposes. While knowledge seekers may be accustomed to a weak grasp of the processes that facilitate their research, this black-boxed technology represents a double-bind and a further testament to objective data worship played out in every conceivable arena of society. Needless to say, how data is embraced or rejected is a matter of culturally inscribed tolerances, as big data and AI-driven approaches to knowledge creation and cultural shaping are both disruptors and creators of perceptions of authority, trustworthiness and credibility, as well as the knowledge claims evaluated in the light of this shifting perceptual capital.

In discussing big data in relation to archives, we were interested in approaches that support the potential for data to be re-used and re-analysed in conjunction with other data that may have been collected by unrelated researchers. Such research is facilitated through the use of descriptive metadata, appropriate preservation systems, informed institutional practice and architecture for sharing across institutions to enable discovery by diffuse researchers.

To understand what the digital turn really means for knowledge practices, it has been argued[27] that we must clarify whether big data is genuinely being adopted as a heuristic by academic, governmental and associated actors, or if the 'myth' of 'Big Data'[28] is merely a useful discourse for those whose interests are served by the promulgation of an evangelical 'dataism'.[29] This phenomenon has parallels across society. For example, Williamson analyses how the Hour of Code and Year of Code initiatives saw 'a computational style of thinking' infiltrate schools in the US and UK, which he describes as a style of thinking that 'apprehends the world as a set of computable phenomena'.[30] Williamson draws attention to a deficit of reflexivity amongst advocates of computational approaches to social problems, which obfuscates the 'worldviews, ideologies and assumptions' of the creators of systems for processing data, black-boxing the processes that delimit data use.[31] Berry[32] draws on Fuller[33] in pointing out that the potential for new technologies to produce and reproduce inequalities in society is not simply a matter of a 'digital divide' but is significantly influenced by the commercial roots and market values of much of this *techno-solutionist* innovation.

These developments may be seen as playing out Technopoly's promise of efficiency,[34] which requires standardization, flattening of nuance, decontextualization and depoliticization of data by algorithms. The result of counting everything is that not everything *counts* – not only because developers avoid or fudge corner cases (as we will explore in Chapter 4) but also because the protective practices of practitioners resistant to data sharing can reinforce invisibility. As we show in our discussion of our findings from the KPLEX study, those in roles of knowledge gatekeepers in conventional archival institutions are thoughtful in weighing up the pros and cons of increased exposure, taking a comprehensive view at least preferable to the blinkered perception of the developers who did not consider Facebook data to involve human subjects, for example (a particularly worrisome case study that will be discussed in more detail in Chapter 2). More recently, Facebook has been called upon to release data relating to its role in inciting genocide in Myanmar (a case discussed in Chapter 8), another 'bad practice' example we will return to in this book's conclusion. Representation through data is very often coterminous with the representation of people and identities, and attempts to obscure or protect these identities can be much more challenging that it may seem. At the macro-level, business models based on big data paradigms that assume appropriate safeguards can therefore be blindsided by their failure to prioritize cultural knowledge, including expertise in minority languages. The stakes, we assert, are too high when the pendulum of risk swings between genocide and the extinction of language. Big data and AI development trajectories are leaving countries with less internationally popular languages, such as Iceland, Latvia and many others, without access to the kinds of linguistic technologies that might enable them to balance the desire to preserve their cultural traditions with acting and competing in a globalized world. What *does* get shared and used is then also important (and potentially harmful) because of its eclipsing effect. Facebook drew attention to its tacit acknowledgement of this social fact by its actions in India, where the company demonstrated *computational thinking* by treating an entire country as an A/B test for its Internet.org project (and this in a country whose residents' lives are already subject to the social sorting behemoth of Aadhaar, a Kafkaesque tech-caste system). We explore such issues of power and the dangers of technology companies being allowed to behave as nation states in Chapter 6.

As the takeover of our knowledge commons by commercial interests becomes more and more an accepted norm, dangerous levels of skewing our information environment is made possible by the extremes of cannibalistic AI journalists[35] and data voids. Siri and Google Assistant are supposed to answer all our questions as long as they mainly relate to what the weather is currently doing, or obey an implicit or explicit script related to increasing or enhancing our role as consumers. Solutions will always be provided but not necessarily ones that answer our original question. The iconography of a magnifying glass is often used for search engines but this tool works in the opposite way to search algorithms, whose powerful position in narrowing horizons of information discovery is discussed in Chapter 5. It is increasingly difficult for knowledge seekers to retain a sense of themselves outside of a paradigm that was heralded with the promise of democratization of knowledge, as only an elite few have the means to work with and control big data.

The above is not to say that we are advocates of calling up Bill Gates to switch the internet off. We are living in the After Google era and pointing at genies we might have wished to remain in their bottles is not our concern. What we do think is worthy of deeper consideration and analysis are the challenges society faces as big data logics collide with our established, valued and essential cultural norms and values. Though technology is itself also a part of culture, when it changes too fast or for too few, it becomes out of step with the identities of too many to support cohesion, displacing the old not in the sense of an organic assimilation, but as a rupture that creates fast-changing classes of epistemic 'haves' and 'have nots'. Over the next seven chapters, we focus on sites of these tensions that may be seen as flashpoints for our relationships with data, knowledge and perhaps even with truth, to better understand the landscape of knowledge *solutions*, and the questions we should be asking.

Applying the KPLEX approach to these issues

These issues, and many others, will be expanded upon over the course of the next seven chapters, drawing together the existing basis of science and technology work with the culturally attuned perspective and results of the KPLEX project. The chapters will look at language, discourse and narrative (Chapter 2), sensemaking in the data-driven age (Chapter 3), the unintentional exposure and silencing of perspectives (Chapters 4–6), and how these trends drive power relations (Chapter 7). In the concluding chapter (Chapter 8), we will return to the high-level questions of culture and how big data development operates within epistemic, organizational and regional cultures, and the opportunities that might lie in this perspective to address some of the tensions and conflicts – individual, ethical and others – that the trouble with data has caused. The book incorporates a tension between the need to focus on culture and cultural practices being datafied or otherwise shaped by data practices, and our wider interest in knowledge creation, data and truth, and the many actors active in this ecosystem.

The book's contribution to developing a language and method for applying humanistic methodologies and knowledge to the problem of big data as a knowledge technology will be laid out as follows:

Chapter 2 begins at the surface level, looking at how language and communication about and around big data research, both scientific and corporate, can be seen to mislead or, at best, fail in its intended purpose to build consensus around what is happening in the 'black box'. Chapter 3 introduces the social dimension of knowledge creation processes and explains two aspects of why big data can be understood as a disruptive force: (a) big data analyses in private corporations are mostly cut off from state-funded scientific communities and therefore from society as such and (b) where the mechanisms used in AI applications to analyse big data are unknown, knowledge creation processes become non-transparent.

The topic of Chapter 4 is resource discovery and search engines, such as Google, which have become the predominant method by which we access knowledge in our daily lives. However, the long tail of Web pages resultant from a keyword query will obfuscate unique research resources for the cultural heritage researcher. For the custodians of the original big data, the cultural heritage institutions, this new discovery mechanism also represents a challenge. They must not only ensure their users discover what is in their holdings but also understand how to expose the context and the tacit knowledge held by cultural heritage practitioners. As cultural heritage practice moves into the digital realm, Chapter 5 examines what other aspects may further lead to data becoming hidden from the historical record and the risks involved in making some data discoverable on-line. How the recently created data and research infrastructure can aid resource discovery for both institutions and their communities is also considered.

The dominant messages surrounding big data often neglect the complexities of people in the process, eliding human contributions to position the outputs of datafication centre stage. Chapter 6 looks at where datafication discourse may take our relationship with complex knowledge, and the historical record itself, by examining its impacts on the practices of archival practitioners and knowledge seekers. We show how big data precepts' crossover to the cultural realm is an example of how deference to human reasoning is being displaced, to the extent that AI might determine what we learn from the historical record, setting a troubling precedent.

Chapter 7 elaborates how big data approaches marginalize culture – here: language, cultural heritage, the culture of scientific knowledge creation – and explains how cultural commons have become transformed into big data which can be exploited by private companies, a development which has to be resisted. Finally, in Chapter 8, we return to the macro-level to open up the question of how a cultural frame of reference might be further extended to serve the project of ensuring that datification processes remain in line with the public good, rather than favouring in such a monocular fashion the imperatives of engineers and the companies that employ them. We conclude with the proposal of one such mechanism, utilizing an intercultural studies approach to frame a new metaphor for the relationship between the users and creators of big data systems. With this provocation and the evidence that proceeds it, we hope to have succeeded in the goal of empowering both researchers and their subjects to make the development of big data approaches to knowledge creation more humane.

Notes

1   Henrich, Joseph, Steven J. Heine and Ara Norenzayan, 'The Weirdest People in the World?', *Behavioral and Brain Sciences*, 33/2–3 (2010), 61–83.
2   Drucker, Johanna, *Speclab* (Chicago: University of Chicago Press, 2009), 27.
3   'ENUMERATE Core Survey 2 (2014) Full Dataset – Excel Format – ENUMERATE Data Platform', https://pro.europeana.eu/files/Europeana_Professional/Projects/ Project_list/ENUMERATE/raw%20data/ENUMERATE_datasheet%202017%20 download.xlsx. See also http://pro.europeana.eu/files/Europeana_Professional/ Projects/Project_list/ENUMERATE/deliverables/DSI-2_Deliverable%20D4.4_ Europeana_Report%20on%20ENUMERATE%20Core%20Survey%204.pdf.
4   'ENUMERATE Core Survey 2 (2014) Full Dataset – Excel Format – ENUMERATE Data Platform', https://pro.europeana.eu/files/Europeana_Professional/Projects/ Project_list/ENUMERATE/raw%20data/ENUMERATE_datasheet%202017%20 download.xlsx.
5   'Europeana Foundation | Europeana Pro', https://pro.europeana.eu/about-us/ foundation.
6   *Directive 2013/37/EU of the European Parliament and of the Council of 26 June 2013 Amending Directive 2003/98/EC on the Re-Use of Public Sector Information Text with EEA Relevance*, 175, 2013 http://data.europa.eu/eli/dir/2013/37/oj/eng.
7   European Commission, 'Draft European Open Science Agenda', 2016, https:// ec.europa.eu/research/openscience/pdf/draft_european_open_science_agenda. pdf#view=fit&pagemo%20de=none.
8   Warwick, Claire, Melissa Terras, Paul Huntington, Nikoleta Pappa and Isabel Galina, *The LAIRAH Project: Log Analysis of Digital Resources in the Arts and Humanities Final Report to the Arts and Humanities Research Council* (School of Library, Archive, and Information Studies, September 2006), 60.

9 Edmond, Jennifer, 'How Scholars Read Now: When the Signal Is the Noise', *Digital Humanities Quarterly* 12/1 (2018).

10 Hall, Bud L., 'Beyond Epistemicide: Knowledge Democracy and Higher Education' (presented at the International Symposium on Higher Education in the Age of NeoLiberalism and Audit Cultures, University of Regina, 2015), https://dspace. library.uvic.ca/bitstream/handle/1828/6692/Hall_Budd_BeyondEpistemicide_2015. pdf?sequence=2&isAllowed=y.

11 As represented in work such as: Liu, Alan, 'Where Is Cultural Criticism in the Digital Humanities?', *Debates in the Digital Humanities*, http://dhdebates.gc.cuny. edu/debates/text/20; Hall, Gary, 'The Digital Humanities beyond Computing: A Postscript', *Culture Machine*, 12 (2011), https://culturemachine.net/wp-content/ uploads/2019/01/11-Digital-Humanities-441-894-1-PB.pdf.

12 Edmond, Prof. dr. J. (Trinity College Dublin) (2018): Knowledge Complexity. DANS, https://doi.org/10.17026/dans-xe6-hpm5. All further references in this book to the KPLEX interviews will be referenced as follows (WPx INTy), where x refers to the workpackage that created the original interview and y refers to the interview number within that group.

13 Surgisphere, an American healthcare analytics company, provided datasets used for studies of Covid-19 that were published in *The Lancet* and *The New England Journal of Medicine* in May 2020. The analysis presented in *The Lancet* claimed to show that patients taking the anti-malaria drug hydroxychloroquine were more likely to die in hospital, prompting the World Health Organization to halt global trials of the drug for use in treating Covid-19 patients, before closer scrutiny revealed serious doubts about the data's provenance. The studies were retracted.

14 GCSE, A level and (Scottish) higher students in the UK did not sit exams in 2020 because schools were closed to most students in response to Covid-19. In England, teachers were asked to supply the official exam regulator, Ofqual, with an estimated grade and ranking for each pupil in all their subjects. These grades and rankings were then subject to an algorithm, which also factored in the school's previous performance, with the aim of allocating grades consistent with schools' prior achievements. The release of results prompted a public outcry, not least because the algorithm could be seen to 'downgrade' state school students, compared to those attending privately funded independent schools, a bias attributed to cohort size. As well as its implications for ideas of equal opportunities and social mobility, this system clearly undermined concerted individual effort. After his administration allowed some appeals resulting in upgrading, Prime Minister Boris Johnson told students: 'I am afraid your grades were almost derailed by a mutant algorithm.' The National Education Union (NEU) called Johnson's comments a 'brazen' attempt to 'idly shrug away a disaster that his own government created'. Coughlan, Sean,

26 August 2020, A-levels and GCSEs: Boris Johnson blames 'mutant algorithm' for exam fiasco https://www.bbc.com/news/education-53923279.

15 Leonelli, Sabine, 'What Difference Does Quantity Make? On the Epistemology of Big Data in Biology', *Big Data & Society*, 1/1 (2014), https://doi.org/10.1177/2053951714534395.

16 Bernstein's (1973) term 'educational knowledge code' describes the set of principles that shape and define a particular discipline, demonstrating its distinct identity among other disciplines and setting boundaries for its curricula, appropriate forms of pedagogy and the means of evaluating teaching and learning.

17 Haraway, Donna, 'Situated Knowledges: The Science Question in Feminism and the Privilege of Partial Perspective', *Feminist Studies*, 14/3 (1988), 575–99.

18 Star, Susan Leigh, 'Power, Technology and the Phenomenology of Conventions: On Being Allergic to Onions', *The Sociological Review*, 38/1 (1990), 26–56.

19 Leonelli, Sabina, 'What Counts as Scientific Data? A Relational Framework', *Philosophy of Science* 82/5 (1 December 2015), 810–21.

20 Haraway, Donna, *When Species Meet* (Minneapolis: University of Minnesota Press, 2008).

21 Leonelli, 'What Counts as Scientific Data? A Relational Framework', 810–21.

22 Ribes, D. and S. J. Jackson, 'Data Bite Man: The Work of Sustaining a Long Term Study', in *'Raw Data' Is an Oxymoron* (Cambridge, MA: MIT Press, 2013), 147–66.

23 McPherson, Tara, 'Why Are the Digital Humanities So White?' in *Debates in the Digital Humanities* (Minneapolis: University of Minnesota Press, 2012).

24 Broadfield, A., *The Philosophy of Classification* (London: Grafton, 1946), 65–6.

25 Daelen, Veerle Vanden, Jennifer Edmond, Petra Links, Mike Priddy, Linda Reijnhoudt, Václav Tollar et al., 'Sustainable Digital Publishing of Archival Catalogues of Twentieth-Century History Archives', 2015, https://hal.inria.fr/hal-01281442; Borgman, C.L., *Big Data, Little Data, No Data: Scholarship in the Networked World* (Cambridge, MA: MIT Press, 2015).

26 Susskind, Richard and Daniel Susskind, *The Future of the Professions. How Technology Will Transform the Work of Human Experts* (Oxford: Oxford University Press, 2015).

27 Bolin, G. and J. Andersson Schwarz, 'Heuristics of the Algorithm: Big Data, User Interpretation and Institutional Translation', *Big Data & Society*, 2/2 (2015), https://cyberleninka.org/article/n/311316; Kitchin, Rob, 'Big Data, New Epistemologies and Paradigm Shifts', *Big Data & Society*, 1/1 (2014), 2053951714528481.

28 boyd, danah and Kate Crawford, 'Critical Questions for Big Data', *Information, Communication & Society*, 15/5 (2012), 662–79.

29 van Dijck, Jose, 'Datafication, Dataism and Dataveillance: Big Data between Scientific Paradigm and Ideology', *Surveillance & Society*, 12/2 (2014), 197–208.

30 Williamson, Ben, 'Political Computational Thinking: Policy Networks, Digital Governance and "Learning to Code"', *Critical Policy Studies*, 10/1 (2016), 39–58.

31 Williamson, 'Political Computational Thinking: Policy Networks, Digital Governance and "Learning to Code"'.

32 Berry, David, 'The Computational Turn: Thinking about the Digital Humanities', *Culture Machine*, 12 (2011), 23.

33 Berry, D. M., 'Humanity: The Always Already – or Never to Be – Object of the Social Sciences?', in *The Social Sciences and Democracy* (London: Palgrave, 2010).

34 Postman, Neil, *Technopoly: The Surrender of Culture to Technology* (New York: Penguin Random House, 1993).

35 Waterson, Jim, 'Microsoft's Robot Editor Confuses Mixed-Race Little Mix Singers', *The Guardian* (9 June 2020), section Technology, http://www.theguardian.com/technology/2020/jun/09/microsofts-robot-journalist-confused-by-mixed-race-little-mix-singers.

2

What do we mean when we talk about data?

'The people who get to impose their metaphors on the culture get to define what we consider to be true.'[1]

How we speak about complicated things matters. The words we choose (or are encouraged to choose) shape not only how we interact with others but also how we ourselves perceive the things we speak of. Language shapes our emotional responses, how we assimilate and organize new information. This is true in particular in terms of our relationship to digital technology, which changes fast, may be hard for non-experts to understand the function of, is often invisible and is central to our lives. Using metaphors to embed technologies into our lives is a process as old as technology development, and we can certainly find recognition of the importance of this process in work such as David Edge's 1974 study 'Technological Metaphor and Social Control'.[2] More recently (in the context of the internet) Sally Wyatt commented:

> Metaphors not only help us to think about the future; they are a resource deployed by a variety of actors to shape the future … Metaphors can mediate between structure and agency, but it is actors who choose to repeat old metaphors and introduce new ones. Thus, it is important to continue to monitor the metaphors at work to understand exactly what work it is that they are doing.[3]

This chapter will look into the implications of this phenomenon as they relate to our relationship with both the idea and reality of data in our lives: a complex, interesting and indeed fraught set of interactions driven only in part by the manner in which the fantasy of data seems to have established itself as a contemporary fetish object, touted as 'the new oil' or even (as one particularly astonishing 2015 advertising campaign launched by the investment company Winton Capital proposed) as the 'secret to living happily ever after'.[4] It is also a danger zone where ephemeral details about our lives and selves may be lost, stolen, sold and ultimately used to exploit us. So fundamental is our dysfunctional relationship with the concept of data that even though talk of it seems to be everywhere, there is not even consensus about whether the word should be used as a singular (as in 'data is') or plural (the grammatically correct, but less commonly used form, 'data are').

The language used in the European General Data Protection Regulation (GDPR) provides a foundation for beginning to understand what data might be from the point of view of an individual. The GDPR defines three different roles related to data regulation: the data subject (a living person who is either identified or identifiable in data), the data controller (a person, company or other body which decides the purposes and methods of processing personal data) and the data processor (a person, company or other body which processes personal data on behalf of a data controller).[5] In Western societies, we are generally accultured to believe that we somehow own what we create: if you bake a cake, you may sell or eat or give it away. It would be generally considered theft for anyone else to do these things to your cake without your permission. If you do harm, you should take responsibility and redress the ill effects of your actions. But this is not the case as pertains to your data: you may feel that you own it, but according to the regulations (and indeed according to many questionable legal instruments you may have signed) you are a data subject, not a controller, or indeed an owner.

This is not merely a bit of legal language intended to control existing relationships between individuals, governments, institutions and companies, however, as what our data 'say' about us is more than a form of personal expression. Marketers on some level realize this, even as they try to ensure we see the positive sides of technology and overlook the threats. As the representative of a company that advocates the move from the 'Internet of Things' (IoT) to the 'Internet of Me' (IoMe) explains: 'Now imagine tech working in your body at the biological level. Your body could express itself on its own, without you having to be in charge, to deliver more happiness, better health, whatever you truly need and want.'[6] Seen this way, your personal data seems to transcend even the idea of free speech to take the place of free will. But even far short of this techno-utopian vision we can find challenges in the idea of personal data being personal in terms of ownership, rather than representation. Whether or not selling our personal data would be akin to selling our autonomy (as Morozov, argued already in 2014);[7] the implications of how we view our agency over the record of our actions, decisions and indeed our biology are wide ranging, because at the end of the day, privacy is a public good. This has been established as a legal precedent,[8] but in the years since that publication plenty of illustrations of precisely how this concept operates in practice have emerged, from revealing the location of US military bases via data from the Strava fitness app[9] to the use of openly shared genomic data, gathered with the intention of learning about one's heritage, to solve cold murder cases.[10]

The semantic gymnastics according to which we co-create data with a variety of places, devices and platforms will be discussed below. But at the heart of the difficulty we have with our personal data is the fact that very often, it is a by-product of other activities. We undertake a Google search with the intention of answering a question or finding information – we do not intend to produce data and may not even be aware that this is precisely what we are doing. We order from Amazon with the intention of getting stuff, we register with Tinder with the intention of finding a partner, we carry our phone in our pocket so that we may be contacted wherever we are. We create data via each of these mundane activities, just as we create carbon dioxide by breathing, but (also like carbon dioxide) we can neither see nor ourselves reuse the data we create, so we tend to ignore them and any implications they may have for our lives. It is this status as what Shoshona Zuboff calls 'behavioural surplus'[11] that makes them so easy for us to ignore, and for companies to exploit. Because we cannot 'see' data, we struggle to understand their size, their presence, their implications. An image search for the word 'data' demonstrates how narrowly our imagination is constrained: numbers and swirls dominate, as do various shades of blue and black.

The demonstrative nature of this example is upheld by research into images used to represent data in two prominent on-line newspapers (*The New York Times* and *The Washington Post*).[12] Images classified there found a reliance on similar forms of abstraction (large-scale numbers, abstract data visualizations, devices, screens, servers, etc.). They also noted the general homogeneity of images beyond these 'curated' media, and also the emphasis on the colour blue. Visually, we have not moved much beyond the compelling image established in the Matrix film series, with a moody Keanu Reeves standing enigmatically in front of scrolling green characters on a black screen, so reminiscent of early monochrome computer monitors

Our vocabulary may not be much more advanced than our visual language for giving shape to data, and indeed the extent to which it is richer may even point towards an even greater weakness. Indeed, the linguistic metaphors we use to refer to data have been the object of a significant body of research, resulting in an interesting overall taxonomy of terms we use to express this seemingly ephemeral, mobile, invisible, but high impact product. The most significant categories of image are those of fluidity (data streams, deluge) and of natural resources (data as oil, data mining)[13] which tend to be divorced from the human-constructedness of data,[14] its personal, embodied and spatial elements – it is (in particular within the 'quantified self' community) a mirror, a practice and a body.[15] Awati[16] adds the categories of surveillance, industry, food and spatial images, while Davenport[17] pinpoints the idea of data as a by-product, of 'data exhaust.' It is interesting how far these metaphors for data are from those Wyatt identified as applying to the internet in 1998: revolution, evolution, salvation, progress, universalism and the 'American dream'.[18]

The language we are encouraged to use in the process of creating this valuable residue stresses the harmlessness of the transactions: we are asked to 'accept cookies' and adjust our 'sharing' settings as a means to imply positive and safe interactions, which are in fact fraught with complexities behind their innocuous linguistic wrappings. These metaphors, at every level, 'are thus not only descriptive; they may provide clues to the design intentions of those who use them and, as such, they may help to shape the cognitive framework within which such actors operate. ... they can be used to help the imaginary become real or true'.[19] In other words, metaphors are not merely effective because of their representational capacity (although this helps) but because the users forget that they are metaphors at all, sublimating them instead as 'embodied cognition'[20] or 'conceptual memory theory'[21] to become a factor that constructs as well as defines the world. Unfortunately, however, it seems inevitable that the level and nature of this 'harmlessness' are defined by – and the profits derived from any inherent risks or costs they may hide being accepted, largely accruing to – corporations selling products and governments engaging in surveillance. These topics will be taken up in more detail in Chapter 6 and 7.

So how should we view our data? Are platforms and services like those provided by Google and Facebook more like utilities we require for daily life, hospitals where we are vulnerable and exposed, cornerstones of democratic exchange? More provocatively, in terms of constitutional protections from warrantless search, is your car like your home, or is your cell phone like your body? Controlling how data are used and how they frame our lives may mean that we need to better control how we speak about them. To many, the resistance to data-driven 'surveillance capitalism'[22] represents a backward-looking denial of the benefits of technology, but one can also view it as a linguistic project to update our metaphors for both our technologies and our identities as they are shaped by them.

No matter how data subjects and producers may imagine and speak of their data, there is no doubt that multibillion dollar companies like Acxiom very much recognize the value of all of these assets, as does Facebook, Google and a host of other companies, governments and other actors. A series of 2018 advertisements for the credit reporting company Experian took an almost cynical approach to what they deemed the 'data self'. 'Your Data Self is the version of you that companies see when you apply for things like credit cards, loans and mortgages.' It said 'You two should get acquainted.'[23] What data are and mean to this company, however, may be very different from how you might see things – indeed, the activities undertaken by companies in the name of product innovation have at times given rise to a host of unexpected consequences (from clickbait content farms in Macedonia to social unrest in Myanmar). Had these companies been held to the ethical codes of the social science researchers they are acting as, or indeed to those present in other industries, like pharmaceuticals, where products sold might be detrimental to health, the landscape of data privacy and reuse might be very different today.

Needless to say, the most well-documented overstepping of ethical lines by a company seeking to obtain data from and about its users has been the 2014 Facebook emotional contagion testing.[24] In this infamous study, the company monitored the effect of subtle tweaks on their algorithm that altered the emotional tone of content viewed by ca. 700,000 of their users. As a result, at the end of a week of this manipulation of their newsfeeds, those same users seemed themselves to post more positively or negatively according to what they had been shown. While it may seem that the question of what responsibility a company has to the users of its service might seem very far from the issues of language at the heart of this chapter, indeed, metaphors are never far from sight. As Hwang and Levy describe the core issues of the case:

> The debate around the emotional contagion experiment, for instance, is fundamentally a debate about what metaphor should guide our thinking about what the Facebook News Feed actually is. As Jeff Hancock, a co-author of the paper based on the experiment, has recognized, '[T]here's no stable metaphor that people hold for what the News Feed is.' Proving the point, commentators have deployed a range of conflicting metaphors to argue about whether the experiment crossed the line: the experimental manipulation has been compared to a field study, to an A/B test, to books and television programs, and even to a dime left suggestively in a public phone booth. The controlling metaphor defines the moral burden of the project: If the contagion experiment is like any other routine A/B test, then there is no foul. If the contagion experiment is more, say, like a field study, it implies a greater ethical onus on the researchers' conduct.[25]

Ethnographer Mary Grey echoes this focus on the language we use to describe what Facebook was doing: 'If researchers or systems designers are "just" testing a product on end users (aka humans) and another group has access to all that luscious data, whose ethics apply? When does "testing" end and "real research" begin in the complicated world of "The Internet?"'[26] The implications of the publication of the research results of Facebook's experiment clearly resonated for the editorial board of the journal presenting the work as well, leading them to add an annex to the paper defending their decision to present the research, but maintaining the caveat that 'it is nevertheless a matter of concern that the collection of the data by Facebook may have involved practices that were not fully consistent with the principles of obtaining informed consent and allowing participants to opt out'.[27] The verbal gymnastics around whether or not Facebook is a 'media company' or just a 'tech company' in the years since this case became public seem to imply that they feel the metaphors are still in their favour. And, indeed, Facebook has only in 2020 set up an independent oversight board[28] for its activities – or so it says. Although the Board does include a number of Facebook's critics and has a statutory independence from the company, its remit is very narrowly proscribed indeed, to cases in which users believe their content has been removed in error or unfairly.

Another place in which the linguistic slipperiness of the business models based on data can be seen is in the ubiquitous terms of service prospective users are asked to agree to. Terms of Service statements very often govern what claims a service provider may make to track, use and resell evidence regarding an individual's behaviour on their platform and beyond. They may purport to being a tool for establishing the rights and responsibilities of both user and service provider; yet, they fail spectacularly to fulfil this function. Social or psychological contracts (based on unwritten, normed expectations, rather than formal, legal instruments) negotiated around the collection and application of technologies based upon big data often demonstrate a core attribute of misunderstanding or miscommunication. In their book *Reengineering Humanity*, Selinger and Frischman bring their perspectives spanning business, law and philosophy together to explore the validity and purpose of these contracts. As such, they raise a large number of concerns about the contents and prevalence of such instruments, deeming them 'oppressive' and based – by design – on the 'irrational' proposition that users might actually read them. From their length to the heuristics of their design to the nature and object of the consent they extract, these so-called contracts represent not only a dramatic change in the number of legal instruments we are expected to engage with in the course of an adult life (from a few in the course of decades to that same number in weeks or days or, potentially, minutes) to the ultimate end of a commodification of users through 'pseudo-relationships'.[29] This brings us back to the need for a stable functional or descriptive definition of data to enable the management of activities with regards to this thing we can neither see nor touch, but which can perhaps be useful or harmful. But finding this clear definition to help us navigate through the obscurity of a data-driven world is also anything but simple.

If we turn for a concrete definition to the vast corpus of material produced within the field of Science and Technology Studies (STS), we find the contentious nature of the space occupied by the word data to be seemingly confirmed. In fact, even between two of the most prominent voices in this chorus, we learn that data has a 'pre-analytical, pre-factual status' that 'resists analysis',[30] and yet ' ... may be facts, sources of evidence, or principles of an argument that are used to assert truth or reality'.[31] This direct contradiction between the (possibly) factual and the pre-factual is par for the course within this particular area of interest and comment, however, as we can easily find as well that data is/are 'rhetorical',[32] 'fiction ... illusion',[33] 'a sort of actor'[34] and/or 'performative'.[35] It/ they 'has no truth',[36] 'resists analysis' and 'cannot be questioned'.[37] This polysemy not only makes it hard to understand the place of data in sensemaking processes (the topic of the next chapter) but also seems to lend to data a certain quality of agency, as in Garvey's statement that data 'will out'.[38] In particular, and equally unusefully, many of the most concrete definitions of data focus less on what they might be and more on what data lack, such as meaning or value, it being unorganized, unprocessed, pre-epistemic, etc.[39]

Of the many definitions for the word data that exist, one of the most useful is surely that posed by Sabina Leonelli. For her, data is a 'relational category applied to research outputs that are taken, at specific moments of inquiry, to provide evidence for knowledge claims of interest to the researchers involved'.[40] For Leonelli, data is not a fixed thing in itself, but a 'portable object', and a means for communication that relies heavily on the observer to attribute meaning to it. With this approach, she manages to demonstrate how data itself is like a language, the components of which can act as evidence for different phenomena from different perspectives at different times, something we cannot view properly when it is divorced from its starting and endpoints, its sources and functions. This points towards the issue of data and its context, which the discussion returns to below.

One of the further factors complicating our search for firm ground with regards to speaking about data is the slippery relationship between data and some of its semantic near neighbours, in particular, 'information' and 'knowledge' (the three of which, together with wisdom, make up the 'DIKW pyramid', 'one of the fundamental, widely recognized and "taken-for-granted" models in the information and knowledge literatures.')[41] Like many such broadly applied models, there is a lot of variation in the application of DIKW and in particular in how the terms that comprise it are seen to be related, except for the fact that they are seen to stand in a hierarchical relationship to each other: that is, that each component of the model acts as a sort of raw material for transforming into the next. This fundamental assumption seems to have been a part of the model from the beginning, appearing already in the paper by Ackoff so many cite as having introduced it, in which he states that each of the higher types in the hierarchy 'includes the categories that fall below it.'[42] The hierarchical nature of the model is problematic, however, seen from the contemporary perspective of how information objects actually circulate. For example, a philosophical treatise may be said to contain wisdom, or at least a record of knowledge, but when it is digitally imaged, transcribed and federated into a digital collection, it then becomes data again. Interesting in this context is the NASA EOSDIS standard for the description of enhancements to data. Like the discussion of DIKW, the framework proposes a number of additions and transformations that may be added to an original dataset, each of which may cause it to then be considered to have reached another level of preparation and refinement. And yet, when that same, now highly processed data is passed to a new use case or context, it reverts in that context back to having a preparation status of level 0 in the framework.[43] This seems also to have been recognized by Carlisle, who states that 'given the idea that information consists of augmented data, then information should possess all of the characteristics of its contributing data, plus additional characteristics. However, since information fails to include the characteristics of existing in time and space, stating that information emerges as a summation of all contributing data entities seems to be a misnomer.'[44]

Whether or not the hierarchical nature of relationships between data, information, knowledge and wisdom is considered to be linear or fluid, the fact of there being any hierarchical or even clear distinctions between them seems refuted by the very linguistic practices of those who write about them (the present authors not necessarily excluded!), creating not only tautologies and chiasms in usage (as, for example, in the statement: '[A researcher states that] in 2006, the world created 161 exabytes of **data** and forecasts that between 2006 and 2010, the **information** added annually to the digital universe will increase more than six fold].'[45] Other definition practices are additive, stating for example: 'Data is the most basic level; Information adds context; Knowledge adds how to use it; Wisdom adds when and why to use it.'[46] Or, more succinctly, the proposal that the four forms equate to 'knownothing', 'knowwhat', 'knowhow' and 'knowwhy', respectively.[47] Indeed, perhaps the most defining characteristic underlying how these key terms will be defined is the disciplinary context any particular author happens to bring to the discussion, be that data science, information science or knowledge management (there is, to our knowledge, no discipline that names itself after or approaches the challenge of understanding knowledge creation from the perspective of wisdom).

The word data seems to obscure itself in any number of ways: through its grammatical form, its semantic complements, its malleability. Even its Latin roots have been called into question as a basis for speaking of the phenomena it proposes to represent. Johanna Drucker has therefore proposed that we should be speaking not of data (from the word 'to give') but of capta (from the word 'to take'):

> Differences in the etymological roots of the terms data and capta make the distinction between constructivist and realist approaches clear. *Capta* is 'taken' actively while *data* is assumed to be a 'given' able to be recorded and observed. From this distinction, a world of differences arises. Humanistic inquiry acknowledges the situated, partial, and constitutive character of knowledge production, the recognition that knowledge is constructed, *taken*, not simply given as a natural representation of pre-existing fact.[48]

No matter what it may be or how one might tacitly or explicitly define it, data are never neutral, never natural phenomena, never 'given'. It is as when Suzanne Briet writes of the difference between an object and its documentation[49] or Greg Crane of the 'digital incunabula',[50] even when there are potentially strong links and relationships between natural phenomena (such as temperature readings or pollutant levels in the air) and their documentations as data, this close relationship does not mean that we can or should ignore their status as 'always already' epistemically marked by the humans who created the measurement protocols, designed the sensors and determined their placement and use (again, an issue we revisit in the next chapter). Instead, if we are to take the position that data function primarily as our personal pre-epistemic 'stuff' (regardless of however processed they may have been by someone else for a different purpose), then we must at least use a term for them that reminds us of their constructedness, and their status within the context into which we import them.

One would hope that where theory fails us, the practices of experts might lead. For this reason, one of the aspects of the cultural underpinnings of software production the KPLEX project interviews probed was how a group of computer scientists used the word data, how they defined it, and what their own habits of thought and speech might tell us about how to improve those of software users. After being given the chance to present their research in their own words and on their own terms, participants were asked how they would define the word data as it pertained to their own work.

The word data was defined as 'text' (WP2 INT1), 'stored information that I can manipulate, search, query, get some statistics about' (WP2 INT2), 'anything that I am analysing, or using to train a system' (WP2 INT4), 'any material that you have in hand ... like digital material' (WP2 INT3), 'everything that I can use to study a certain subject' (WP2 INT5), information that could be quantified. ... that you would use (WP2 INT7), any piece of information that ... can be recorded in an index, 'just evidence' (WP2 INT9), or 'any piece of information, literally anything, but if you're looking for a computer science point of view, any structured bit of information is data' (WP2 INT8). The tendency to view data as something almost transcendently broad was perhaps best summarized in the statement 'data exists, it does exist, it just exists in and of itself' (WP2 INT6).

The clear trend running throughout these examples points towards an epistemic cultural bias towards viewing data, whatever it is, as broadly encompassing, and in terms of its function or utility in the research project, rather than a complex set of information objects that come with biases built in to them, and which might merit a certain amount of meta-reflection. Data, in other words, means 'stuff'. As a side note, it is also interesting to observe that almost all of the respondents used the word 'data' in the singular, a habit of thought that seems to underline this apparent bias against constraining the nature, status and role of data in their work.

Perhaps all the more interesting in this context, then, were those individuals for whom the request to define this key term for their work – and there is no question that the term is central, appearing between 50 and 220 times in each sixty- to seventy-five-minute interview – was met with some discomfort or resistance. Two people began their responses with the very honest disclaimers that they either didn't 'have a perfect text definition of data' (WP2 INT8) or that it was 'not clearly defined' for them (WP2 INT13) while another claimed not to use the term to describe any aspect of their work (WP2 INT10). Most striking perhaps in this respect was the following response, in which a computer scientist, who described their general research space as comprising data analytics, knowledge extraction from texts, natural language processing and information retrieval, replied:

I don't think like my opinion is that important. I try to explain what I know. I think of data as ... I just mean that I don't have maybe enough knowledge in the area. I know some things, but there are definitely like way smarter people but I try to give you what I have.

(WP2 INT3)

It is perhaps a humanistic bias to expect expertise to include a precision in language around key terminology, and a few respondents did offer alternative words that they would use instead of data in certain situations, such as 'content' (WP2 INT9), or a 'corpus' (WP2 INT13). The gap in the confidence of these researchers between their ability to work with certain kinds of material and talk about it was, however, striking. As a side note, this tendency stands in interesting contrast to the apparent humanistic resistance of the term 'data', which a fascinating Twitter thread instigated by Miriam Posner in 2018 showed to be perceived as narrow, derived, impoverished, simple or monophonic, perhaps even sinister or indicative that a researcher 'doesn't value [a source] or respect its integrity'.[51]

As a follow-up to the prompt to suggest their own definitions, the participants were presented with some of the STS definitions of data discussed above. The participant reactions were interestingly passionate. In many cases the definitions were deemed potentially or partially true (WP2 INT3) or interesting (WP2 INT7), but many more participants found them 'negative' (WP2 INT3), wrong (WP2 INT2), 'just nuts' (WP2 INT6) only applicable in certain contexts and under certain assumptions (WP2 INT8), contradictory to commonly held understandings (WP2 INT7), or at least very flawed, likely to be based on a 'lack of the understanding of data' (WP2 INT2) or 'anthropomorphising'. Quite a few responses deemed the entire discussion to be too 'philosophical' (WP2 INT4, INT5, INT6), and several participants did not want to engage the question, characterizing their 'opinion' as 'not important' (WP2 INT3) or 'just not as magical' (WP2 INT6) as the STS perspectives seemed to them. The researchers often struggled very openly to come to grips with the STS definitions, evidencing a significant gap between STS and computer science, as can be seen particularly well in this excerpt:

Yeah, I'm surprised by the (definition that data are] false, data is false. I don't, I think I need more context in that one. ... I take data from, like, another, a completely different system and I claim that to be what it's not, that could be false. But it's not the data that is false, it's what you claim about the data that is false. Data has no truth? I don't think that's true. Data, all data, has, they are truth. Even if it's false or not, for example.

(WP2 INT5)

The cultural practices of data usage as both an object of and input to software development are deeply engrained, in particular as pertains to the deeply embedded, contextual understanding of the term 'data'. Data as research object appear(s) as overdetermined and highly volatile within the communities that use it most. As such, these expert user practices are of little use in the development of language-based tools to inculcate more informed equivalents among the general public of data subjects and producers of data by-products: are the data an input or an output? Human or only machine readable? Are they being used transparently, and for the purpose they were gathered? Mary Grey reminds us that how we weight the ethical implications of our activities is highly dependent on how we see our objects of study, whether we believe ourselves to be working with strings of numbers and letters or whether we can see the people and the social interactions behind them.[52]

There is one further thing that these interviews do throw into strong relief, however, an issue that stems directly from how data are viewed and their relationship to the speech acts that surround them, specifically the question of **context**. In order to make and share meaning around a term with no truly fixed referent, one must ensure that the word is instead anchored temporarily for a given purpose, and that there is strong communal agreement around these processes and purposes.

The preservation, disruption or alteration of context both is and isn't a linguistic process: perhaps it would be better to characterize it as a communicative one, and certainly in this respect it is a challenge we face within in our daily lives as consumers and circulators of information. What aspects of one's adventure of a Saturday night might one share with one's best friend, as opposed to one's socially conservative grandmother? What language differences might there be between these two accounts? How might you respond differently to an account of a scientific experiment represented in a research paper, or an interview with a politician, or a post on Facebook from an unknown source (the phenomenon known as 'context collapse'[53])? Context gates the future actionability and credibility of a data signal received: as Christine Borgman described the relationship, '[data] exist in a context, taking on meaning from that context and from the perspective of the beholder. The degree to which those contexts and meanings can be represented influences the transferability of the data.'[54] The many layers to the context that enable this transferability are often sublimated and indeed disregarded in its processing, however, regardless of which of the definitions or models one chooses to ascribe to in coming to terms with the concept of data.

The power of data is strongly, and perhaps ironically, linked to its context. In general, the variety of definitions we looked at above imply that one of the key characteristics of data is that it has been divorced from its originating context and the complexity that would come with it: it is this lack of context that would render it pre-epistemic, pre-factual or resistant to analysis. It is also the characteristic of data that the NASA model explicitly recognizes: when the context of data use changes, so also does its complexity, regardless of what transformations or contextual information it may have previously been enhanced with.[55]

The contextual layer for any given piece or collection of data, were it captured in full, would be complex indeed. If we start with the point at which Drucker identified the rift between data and capta,[56] we can find already a fundamental layer of context, what a historian would probably recognize as resembling the **provenance** of a source, including how a certain intention could create data utterly unrelated to the context later applied to it. Was a Google search about suicide methods motivated by a personal crisis or a writing project? Was a particular location visited in order to walk a dog, buy a doughnut or escape a sense of being followed? Even the most simple scientific data is marked at some level as human produced capta (who designed or manufactured the sensor? Who determined its precise position?), but human behaviour is always complex, and no matter how much data about it is captured, there is always more that is missed. After all, as the refrain reminds us, all models lie (even if some models happen also to be useful).

How and what context is maintained alongside what data have been gathered is complicated by the additional question of what new context has been added, in terms of description, structuring or even of aggregation with other data. This layer denotes a transition from context as a question of provenance to one of **curation** and **information modelling**. Although this former term has its roots in the field of museology, some sort of similar process of filtering, aggregation, refinement, arrangement or enhancement takes place in almost every processing of knowledge. Even the data produced by the Large Hadron Collider undergoes a (human-driven, hard-coded) process of filtering and selection before it is made available to researchers.[57] It is almost inevitable that the capta we collect, be they observations via a telescope or collider, a walk in the park or perusal of manuscript images, will need to be winnowed, aggregated like-with-like and organized in such a way as to represent a reasonable baseline knowledge organization – even more so in our current scientific and human condition of potential information overload. This is not a process to be taken lightly, however. In the age of fake news and alternate facts, the process of curating a dataset should itself be documented and fully proofed for the biases it may enhance, obscure or introduce into the new interpretations this process facilitates. A survey of an interdisciplinary cohort of researchers undertaken by the KPLEX project in order to understand the range of attitudes towards data-driven research and the management practices that underpin it shows a significant lack of consensus regarding how to responsibly balance the limits one's data capture processes and the processability of data for a specific purpose and again it is the terminology used to describe differing processes that tell us most about the risks and gains inherent in them. In particular, the terms 'data cleaning' and 'data manipulation' emerged as descriptors for the same process with very different values implied by them. The latter term was seen as an arbitrary act to make data fit with other data, which seems to have a negative connotation as this email feedback makes clear: 'I doubt it very much that any self-respecting quantitative researcher would admit to manipulating their data! This is what your questions on p. 2 imply'.[58] Data cleaning is seemingly understood as unscientific when handling data, and less so as a necessary step within the processing of data that assures the accuracy, completeness, consistency (and uniformity) of a dataset. In the social and natural sciences on the other hand, more than half of the survey participants perform some sort of data cleaning.[59] This difference in perspectives is reminiscent of what Leonelli describes at the 'journeys' taken by data, passing through research contexts and acquiring and losing aspects of its scaffolding as it is decontextualized, recontextualized and reused.[60]

One of the imperatives often driving the processes of data cleaning (or manipulation) is the need to organize data in order to make them processable. In its simplest format, this may involve populating a table that aligns simple answers to the same question from multiple respondents, but in more complex operations, structured, limited sets of descriptors applying standardized sets of terms known as metadata may be used. This is another processing step where the KPLEX survey exposed significant disagreement between fields, in particular as pertained to the standardized vocabulary for describing emotions (EmotionML) which, in spite of being accepted by the regulatory body W3C, was not widely used in research.[61] While standardization does lead to comparability across datasets and ease of processing, the question remains how much context must be removed, changed or obscured by the strong structuring of a standards-driven information architecture. Metadata can become a determining factor in whether or not an item is returned as a positive or relevant item when the structured data is processed, and the 'raw' (or 'native') data shaped by the database or metadata structure and contexts applied to it.

Although the effects of explicitly applied knowledge organization frameworks will be a focus for later chapters in this book, it is worth noting even at this early point that such descriptions within data systems can have an impact on messages received (even when they are not intended to be 'heard'). Re-contextualization of this sort can undo efforts to anonymize data (in order to protect its subjects), leading to the phenomenon known as 'dark linking', in which proxy data from one source can essentially unmask subjects in another. The problem of data as an instrument for the transfer of the fundamental building blocks for understanding is of course also a problem on the receiver's side of the communication paradigm. The value of knowledge creation processes is often measured according to norms quite distanced from those that give immediate shape to them. Here, no matter how we view this process or the biases it may bring, is where we invariably see the hierarchy perhaps envisioned by the DIKW pyramid converge with that so suspiciously viewed in the KPLEX interviewees (described further in Chapter 3): **narration**. Organized, synthesized, filtered and augmented capta alone will not bring meaning to *homo narrans*. Regardless of what our stories are – the tale of a day's activities or the findings of a research experiment – our communication will be considered flawed unless we bring our knowledge into a temporal framework, into a language of cause and effect, into a story. There is an obvious difference between a chat between friends over dinner and a scientific paper however, in spite of the fact that each of these narratives might reflect roughly the same content and processes: capta, curation and narrative. For that reason, one also needs to consider **performance**. Each of these facets of context, and the many more possible, reflects a specificity not just of what capta or data are relevant, how they might be filtered and what structure might be placed by an individual around them. We perform for an audience, we share our stories and seek to have them validated, thereby valorizing our own epistemic journey, as well as introducing our narratives back into society, so that they themselves might become a source of capta for others. A lack of attentiveness to this social dimension of knowledge creation is what has led to the emergence of the phenomenon known as *context collapse*, which 'problematizes the individual's ability to shift between ... selves and come off as authentic or fake'.[62] Recognizing the performative aspect of science could also contribute to the improvement of public trust in experts, whose narratives of discovery and evidence should be able to contribute to the knowledge of both lay people and fellow experts, but whose performative range may sometimes be too limited to do so.

The possibility obviously exists to maintain all of these contextual layers of data, of making them a part of how we create services, business models and indeed knowledge out of the traces of human activity in the digital age. After all, what is a library or a museum if not an attempt to maintain the objects able to transfer meaning as well as the dense web of contexts that enrich and entangle them (as opposed to a 'data warehouse' where neatly wrapped components wait to be bought and sold)? A number of factors have driven us towards a different paradigm, however – not only technology, but modernity itself, which brought us the 'socialization of statistics'[63] and the rise of 'mechanical objectivity' with its desire to replace human judgement with transcendent 'rules of method, measurement and work discipline'[64] which could transcend the limits of human sensory perception. This trajectory can only be seen as continuing in our current day, where data, as a sort of platonic ideal (what Presner might call a 'data sublime'[65]) for a source of unbiased insight, become portrayed as more accurate and insightful than other information sources.[66]

Just as centuries of mathematics laid the groundwork for the turn towards statistics, this major shift in what was considered objective, credible and robust laid the ground for the knowledge creation that we now see, driven by the availability of massive bodies of data and the algorithmic models able to parse them. If data has become a fetish term, then big data is practically an object of worship, though perhaps one no more strictly defined than its more diminutive precursor.

The tendency to view knowledge objects at every level of epistemic preparation and contextualization as products, rather than human-driven processes, leads to a large number of barriers to the systematic exploration of how knowledge is created by professionals, but also by individuals in their personal lives and contexts. Greater precision of language among the professionals regarding the nature of personal information stored and processed – capta become capital, as it were – could only have a positive effect on the empowerment of individuals in the face of fake news, meaningless consent protocols, filter bubbles and all of the related issues where something perhaps given as data becomes curated into a very different kind of story than we might have expected. The cost of not addressing these gaps is already becoming apparent, as values that have long been a safe haven within democratic systems, like unbiased judgement and free speech, seem somehow to have become suspect. Rehabilitating the idea of the epistemic narrative upon solid ground would be a strong first step in addressing this state of affairs, and of creating both experts and citizens who can speak more clearly about their knowledge environments, processes, outputs and goals. These are the processes we turn to in the following chapters.

Notes

1   Lakoff, George and Mark Johnson, *Metaphors We Live By* (Chicago: University of Chicago Press, 2008).

2   Edge, David, 'Technological Metaphor and Social Control', *New Literary History*, 6/1 (1974), 135–47.

3   Wyatt, Sally, 'Danger! Metaphors at Work in Economics, Geophysiology, and the Internet', *Science, Technology, & Human Values*, 29/2 (2004), 242–61.

4   Edmond, Jennifer and Georgina Nugent Folan, 'Digitising Cultural Complexity: Representing Rich Cultural Data in a Big Data Environment', in *Ways of Being in a Digital Age – A Review Conference* (Liverpool, United Kingdom, 2017), https://hal. archives-ouvertes.fr/hal-01629459.

5   'Art. 4 GDPR – Definitions', *GDPR.Eu*, 2018, https://gdpr.eu/article-4-definitions/

6   Aspell, Ryan, 'The Internet of Me: When the Consumer Becomes the Electronics', *Wired* (8 January 2018), https://www.wired.com/brandlab/2018/01/internet-consumer-becomes-electronics/.

7   Morozov, Evgeny, 'Selling Your Bulk Online Data Really Means Selling Your Autonomy', *The New Republic* (14 May 2014), https://newrepublic.com/article/117703/selling-personal-data-big-techs-war-meaning-life.

8   Fairfield, Joshua A.T. and Christopher Engel, 'Privacy as a Public Good', *Duke Law Journal*, 65/3 (2015), 385–457.

9   Ruser, Nathan, *Twitter*, 2018, https://twitter.com/Nrg8000/status/957318498102865920.

10   Murphy, Heather, 'How an Unlikely Family History Website Transformed Cold Case Investigations – *The New York Times*', 2018, https://www.nytimes.com/2018/10/15/science/gedmatch-genealogy-cold-cases.html.

11   Zuboff, Shoshona, *The Age of Surveillance Capitalism: The Fight for a Human Future at the New Frontiers of Power* (London: Profile, 2019).

12   Pentzold, Christian, Cornelia Brantner and Lena Fölsche, 'Imagining Big Data: Illustrations of "Big Data" in US News Articles, 2010–2016', *New Media & Society*, 21/1 (2019), 139–67.

13   Lupton, Deborah, 'Personal Data Metaphors and Imagery', *This Sociological Life* (2018), https://simplysociology.wordpress.com/2018/10/10/personal-data-metaphors-and-imagery/.

14   Levy, Tim and Karen Hwang, '"The Cloud" and Other Dangerous Metaphors', *The Atlantic* (2015), https://www.theatlantic.com/technology/archive/2015/01/the-cloud-and-other-dangerous-metaphors/384518/.

15   Watson, Sara M., 'Data Is the New "___"', *DIS Magazine,* http://dismagazine.com/discussion/73298/sara-m-watson-metaphors-of-big-data/.

16	Awati, Kailash and Simon Buckingham Shum, 'Big Data Metaphors We Live By', *Towards Data Science*, https://towardsdatascience.com/big-data-metaphors-we-live-by-98d3fa44ebf8.

17	Davenport, Thomas H., 'Who Owns Your Data Exhaust?', *WSJ Magazine* (2013), https://www.wsj.com/articles/BL-CIOB-3319.

18	Wyatt, Sally, 'Danger! Metaphors at Work in Economics, Geophysiology, and the Internet', *Science, Technology, & Human Values*, 29/2 (2004), 251.

19	Ibid., 244.

20	Watson, 'Data Is the New "___"'.

21	Puschmann, Cornelius and Jean Burgess, 'Big Data, Big Questions| Metaphors of Big Data', *International Journal of Communication*, 8/0 (2014), 20.

22	Zuboff, Shoshana, *The Age of Surveillance Capitalism* (London: Profile Books, 2019).

23	McGovern, Laura, 'Experian: Meet Your Data Self', *Laura McGovern* (2018), https://www.lauramcgovern.com/Experian.

24	Kramer, Adam, Jamie Guillory and Jeffrey Hancock, 'Experimental Evidence of Massive-Scale Emotional Contagion through Social Networks', *Proceedings of the National Academy of Sciences of the United States of America*, 111 (2014).

25	Levy and Hwang, '"The Cloud" and Other Dangerous Metaphors'.

26	Gray, Mary L., 'When Science, Customer Service, and Human Subjects Research Collide. Now What?', *Ethnography Matters* (2014), https://ethnographymatters.net/blog/2014/07/07/when-science-customer-service-and-human-subjects-research-collide-now-what/.

27	Kramer, Adam D. I., Jamie E. Guillory and Jeffrey T. Hancock, 'Experimental Evidence of Massive-scale Emotional Contagion through Social Networks', *Proceedings of the National Academy of Sciences*, 111/24 (2014), 8788–90.

28	'Governance | Oversight Board', https://www.oversightboard.com/governance/

29	Frichmann, Brett and Evan Selinger, *Re-Engineering Humanity* (Cambridge: Cambridge University Press, 2018), 60–6.

30	Rosenberg, D., 'Data before the Fact', in *'Raw Data' Is an Oxymoron* (Cambridge, MA: MIT Press, 2013), 18.

31	Borgman, C.L., *Big Data, Little Data, No Data: Scholarship in the Networked World* (Cambridge, MA: MIT Press, 2015), 17.

32	Rosenberg, 'Data before the Fact', 18.

33	Ibid., 3–4.

34	Ribes, D., and S. J. Jackson, 'Data Bite Man: The Work of Sustaining a Long Term Study', in *'Raw Data' Is an Oxymoron* (Cambridge, MA: MIT Press, 2013), 148.

35	Raley, R, 'Dataveillance and Counterveillance', in *'Raw Data' Is an Oxymoron* (Cambridge, MA: MIT Press, 2013), 128.

36	Rosenberg, 'Data before the Fact', 18.

37   Rosenthal, Jesse, 'Introduction: "Narrative against Data"', *Genre*, 50/1 (2017), 1.

38   Garvey, E.G., '"Facts and FACTS:" Abolitionists' Database Innovations', in '*Raw Data*' *Is an Oxymoron* (Cambridge, MA: MIT Press, 2013), 90.

39   Rowley, Jennifer, 'The Wisdom Hierarchy: Representations of the DIKW Hierarchy', *Journal of Information Science*, 33/2 (2007), 171.

40   Leonelli, S., 'What Difference Does Quantity Make? On the Epistemology of Big Data in Biology', *Big Data & Society*, 1/1 (2014), 180.

41   Rowley, 'The Wisdom Hierarchy: Representations of the DIKW Hierarchy', 163–4.

42   Ackoff, R.L., 'From Data to Wisdom', *Journal of Applied Systems Analysis*, 16 (1989), 3.

43   Science Mission Directorate, 'Data Processing Levels', *NASA Science,* https:// science.nasa.gov/earth-science/earth-science-data/data-processing-levels-for-eosdis-data-products.

44   Carlisle, J.P., 'Continuing the DIKW Hierarchy Conversation', Spring (presented at the MWAIS 2015 Proceedings Midwest, 2015), 5.

45   Jifa, G. and Z. Lingling, 'Data, DIKW, Big Data and Data Science', *Procedia Computer Science*, 31 (2014), 815.

46   Jifa and Lingling, 'Data, DIKW, Big Data and Data Science', *Procedia,* 814.

47   Zeleny, Milan, 'Management Support Systems: Towards Integrated Knowledge Management', *Human Systems Management*, 7/1 (1987), 59–70.

48   Drucker, Johanna, 'Humanities Approaches to Graphical Display', *Digital Humanities Quarterly*, 005/1 (2011).

49   Briet, Suzanne, Ronald E. Day, Laurent Martinet and Hermina G.B. Anghelescu, *What Is Documentation? English Translation of the Classic French Text* (Lanham, MD: Scarecrow Press, 2006).

50   Crane, Gregory, David Bamman, Lisa Cerrato, Alison Jones, David Mimno, Adrian Packel et al., 'Beyond Digital Incunabula: Modeling the Next Generation of Digital Libraries', in *Research and Advanced Technology for Digital Libraries*, ed. Costantino Julio Gonzalo, M. Thanos, Felisa Verdejo and Rafael C. Carrasco, Lecture Notes in Computer Science (Berlin, Heidelberg: Springer, 2006), 353–66.

51   Posner, Miriam, *Twitter*, 2018, https://twitter.com/miriamkp/status/ 1057706465866133504.

52   Gray, 'When Science, Customer Service, and Human Subjects Research Collide. Now What?'

53   Marwick, Alice E. and danah boyd, 'I Tweet Honestly, I Tweet Passionately: Twitter Users, Context Collapse, and the Imagined Audience', *New Media and Society*, 13.1.2011.

54   Borgman, *Big Data, Little Data, No Data: Scholarship in the Networked World.*

55   Science Mission Directorate, 'Data Processing Levels', *NASA Science.*

56   Drucker, 'Humanities Approaches to Graphical Display', 17.

57   DARIAH-EU, *Sally Wyatt: 'What Are We Talking about When We Talk about Data in the Humanities?' (DARIAH* 2019), 2019 https://www.youtube.com/watch?v=fmzi X4lHBoc&feature=youtu.be.

58   Edmond, Jennifer, Thomas Stodulka, Elisabeth Huber and Jörg Lehmann, *KPLEX Report on Data, Knowledge Organization and Epistemics* (31 March 2018), 1–118, https://kplexproject.files.wordpress.com/2018/06/k-plex_wp4_report-data-knowledge-organisation-epistemics.pdf.

59   Stodulka, Thomas, 'Emotion Work, Ethnography, and Survival Strategies on the Streets of Yogyakarta', *Medical Anthropology*, 34/1 (2015), 84–97.

60   Leonelli, 'What Difference Does Quantity Make? On the Epistemology of Big Data in Biology'.

61   Stodulka, 'Emotion Work, Ethnography, and Survival Strategies on the Streets of Yogyakarta', *Medical Anthropology*, 34 (2014), 84–97.

62   Marwick, Alice E. and danah boyd, 'I Tweet Honestly, I Tweet Passionately: Twitter Users, Context Collapse, and the Imagined Audience', *New Media & Society*, 13/1 (2011), 114–33.

63   Fienberg, Stephen E., 'A Brief History of Statistics in Three and One-half Chapters: A Review Essay', ed. by Lorraine J. Daston, Gerd Gigerenzer, Zeno Swijtink, Theodore Porter, Lorraine Daston, John Beatty et al., *Statistical Science*, 7/2 (1992), 208–25.

64   Daston, Lorraine J. and Peter Louis Galison, *Objectivity* (New York: Princeton University Press, 2015), 118.

65   Presner, Todd, 'The Ethics of the Algorithm: Close and Distant Listening to the Shoah Foundation Visual History Archive', in *Probing the Ethics of Holocaust Culture* (Cambridge: Harvard University Press, 2016), 175–202.

66   Lupton, Deborah, 'The Thirteen Ps of Big Data', *This Sociological Life* (2015), https://simplysociology.wordpress.com/2015/05/11/the-thirteen-ps-of-big-data/.

3

Making sense of data

'What do the data say?' is one of those questions we might hear more and more often in the offices of executives and data analysts, who aim to make their decisions and develop strategies based on the digital data collected by corporations and through online media. After a second thought, we might answer: 'Well, data don't say anything; they don't speak; they don't have a mouth, and they don't deliver the interpretations on which decisions and strategies are based.' It seems to be an odd feature of our times that data have been bestowed with the status of an oracle who tells us what to do and how to proceed. In this popular view, and in the discursive practices discussed in Chapter 2, data are seen as 'facts', prepared in numerical or textual form, which seem to bear the quality of being authentic and original, objective, pre-interpretive and impartial, guaranteeing value-free description. In contrast to them, the interpretations which are based on them, the sense and meaning we attribute to them, and the narratives we create out of data analysis seem to result from a secondary, additive process which pollutes the authenticity of the original data, making them somehow 'false' and thus 'distorting' an accurate representation of reality. As one person interviewed by the KPLEX project put it:

> I would say that narrative is much more like, that's completely fake. Like, any sort of model or meaning or you know representation or any of these kind of stories that we come up with, they're not an accurate representation of reality, for sure. And as much as possible, people try to use data to back it up, to show that their narrative, their representation of the world is correct.
>
> (WP2 INT6)

The interpretation and narratives produced by humans on the basis of these data imply, in this view, the danger of deformation and misrepresentation, the addition of a potentially false layer, the misdirection of perception and the pollution by the human stain of meaning-making: 'I think the narrative comes after an interpretation of data. So, it's like you look into the data, you give yourself some kind of idea about what's going on. So, it's like yeah you're adding basically, an interpretation, and that of course can be false' (WP2 INT2). But how have we arrived at such a staunch opposition of data and narratives, of 'facts' and 'interpretation'? What kind of facticity is being seen in data, especially in big data, in contrast to the meaning transported by narratives? Which traits and functions differentiate the use of data and narratives? What is the surplus value of interpretation and narrativization, produced by humans, thus laying bare qualities which show that data don't render storytelling obsolete?

Interpretation in the humanities: Two examples

How we use data (and big data) to come to understand the world is not universal or natural, it is a social construction and a cultural process, engaging deeply with values and beliefs as well as language practices. And so, in order to answer these questions, it is necessary to turn away from data science and look at scientific approaches where the fabrication of meaning and the creation of interpretive narratives are part of the daily business and central to the social functions of these disciplines. In the humanities, the methodological approaches of history and literature researchers developed and handed down along generations of scientific practice start from the close inspection and comprehensive scrutiny of data. More often than not, the term 'data' is not used here; rather, historians speak of 'sources' and literature scholars of 'primary material' or 'primary literature'. The use of these terms reflects on the one hand the long-standing traditions of both disciplines and point back to times when the term 'data' was uncommon (as the discussion of this issue in the last chapter has shown). On the other hand, 'data' designates something already processed, while 'sources' or 'primary literature' point to the original, authentic and unaltered material, such as can be found in archives or libraries. Furthermore, such disciplines have developed comprehensive methodologies and prescriptions on how to deal with the materials under scrutiny. In historical research, so-called auxiliary sciences have been established which frame the examination of a whole range of different classes of sources, such as handwritten material in general ('palaeography'), more specifically documents, records, and proceedings or coats of arms, seals and coins. The inspection of these sources always comprises a thorough discussion of source provenance, a reconstruction of the context in which such a source was produced, a critical assessment of the reliability of the source and its explanatory power for a given research question.

Humanistic research processes, in contrast to data-driven ones, are often perceived to be subjective, lacking rigour, or even emotion-driven, but they are nothing of the sort. Historians traditionally visit archives, consult finding aids in order to determine which sources would be valuable for their research project and which are not, and discuss with archivists whether or not there are further sources which might be relevant for their research. They gather research literature in order to determine which sources have already been investigated and thus be part of their scientific endeavour or not. In a next step, historians perform a critical assessment of these sources and take notes on them, a process which often implies the inspection of hundreds or even thousands of different sources. Gaining an overview of the multitude of available sources allows the development of a research hypothesis which is then fostered by at times multiple re-readings of sources, selecting some sources while dismissing others. This comprehensive process of knowledge creation is often reflected in the final product – the research article or monograph – where it may be documented why certain sources have been used while others were not deemed valuable for the analysis. Since historical sources are mostly unique copies and cannot be created ex post (in contrast to the process of data collection), the scarcity of these sources often leads to the phenomenon that the same sources are re-read by different generations of historians. Think of historical evidence from antiquity, where the availability of material is limited and the discovery of new sources, for example, through archaeological excavations, forms the exception rather than the norm. These multiple re-readings of sources reveal a peculiarity common to the humanities, namely the phenomenon that there is no exhaustive interpretation of any source; rather, they can be consulted again and again by different generations of historians re-visiting these sources working on different research questions with a different focus, be it on constructions of gender in earlier times, on manifestations of everyday life, on culturally different forms of handling disputes, on conceptions of space and time, the networks between people or the like. This stands in contrast to the data practices of an organization like CERN, where data volumes can be so large that throwing data away is a normal practice. In history, however, the process of knowledge creation is regarded as never-ending: any particular time will create new questions to be answered by the scrutiny of historical sources.

In the study of literature, the focus is not on unique sources, but on printed books, that is, on technically reproduced material. In traditional literary research, studies most often concentrate on a single work or on the work of a single author. Similar to historical research, the methodology is hermeneutical: a given work is read and re-read multiple times, gathering evidence from the text(s) according to the research question, contextualizing it by cultural and biographical sources or secondary literature, alternative readings of the text and complementary interpretations found in studies published earlier. Since the focus is more on contemporary culture or cultural heritage than on the reconstruction of history, the interdependencies between the text or passages from the text and the surrounding cultural horizons are explored. The methodology, hermeneutics, can be understood as a circumference through subjective comprehension. It is an iterative, self-reflexive process, going back and forth between preconception and understanding, ultimately aiming at interpretation. As such this practice seeks to create not so much a 'black box' as a prismatic one, through which light refracts in different waves. Humanists focus on the exemplary and are not necessarily interested in generalization and exact quantities. A humanist can develop her comprehension of individual authors; her comprehension of the relationship between these single authors and the intellectual contexts they live in; and her comprehension of these intellectual contexts, that is, the larger environment of individuals, the discursive structures or cultural patterns prevailing in the period which is being researched. This methodological process, summarized in the conception of the hermeneutic circle, includes reflections on the conditions determining the structures and patterns which can be found in the text. Moreover, it entails considerations of the limitations imposed by the text – what it can tell and what is not contained – and on the limited range of insights offered by the method. Literary scholars are aware of the social constructedness of meaning in literary products and of the processes of sensemaking peculiar to literature, of the true nature of their data, as it were, as capta, which are brought into dialogue with the cultural context. As such, hermeneutics is opposed to positivism, which is seen to be narrowed to the statements which can be found in a text and which disregards context or regards it as *quantité negligeable*.

In both of these disciplines the hallmarks of the humanities are clearly visible: hermeneutic, critical and speculative thinking, thorough evaluation of the sources, thick description capturing the context, profound understanding of the particular, attentiveness towards meaningful differences.[1] The studies presented by historians and literary scholars ultimately aim at spinning a narrative web that conveys the interpretation elaborated by the researcher. These narratives contain what has been acquired along the way up to the writing of the study: precise observation of details, distinction between relevant and irrelevant information (or 'signal' and 'noise'), complex syntheses, long chains of argumentation, the handling of alterity and particularity. It is not contested that these narratives are the ultimate result of the subjective choices and decisions by the individual researcher, and it is a commonplace that the studies presented by history or literature scholars are subjective: they are themselves placed in the context of their creation, and they entail the use of rhetorical devices and persuasive strategies. However, there is a paradox here in that such studies are nonetheless objective. In order to better understand the subjectivity–objectivity paradox of the humanities, one of the most famous sentences ever written in modern historiography can be cited. In 1885, the German historian Leopold von Ranke defined 'blos zeigen, wie es eigentlich gewesen'[2] as the task of historiography. For a long time, this has been translated as 'merely to show how it really was'. Such an understanding of the occupation of a historian implies that the historian employs a positivistic approach, discovers objective facts and uncovers the truth about the past. But a more appropriate translation would be 'merely to show how it essentially was'; according to this small shift, the task of the historian would therefore be to deliver the essence of the past, an essence that has to be 'distilled' from the sources and might not be directly contained in them. It is obvious that Ranke understood very well that history is a subjective discipline,[3] and he was fully aware of the function of a historian within society. To determine where we come from, who we are, which norms are formative for our behaviour, how history shapes the objectives of our actions and those of institutions, and what the historical record means for the present and the future, all this entails the creation of identities. Or, to present it in another way: if people's understanding of themselves requires history, then identity formation and foundation no longer work without history.

This function of historiography is not specific to the nineteenth century or the historicism of Ranke's time. Another famous German historian, Thomas Nipperdey, began his impressive *Deutsche Geschichte* (published in 1983 for the first time) with the sentence: 'Am Anfang war Napoleon.'[4] Invoking Genesis, German history and identity are described with regard to Napoleon's massive influence on the Germans and in contrast to the major opponent of the Germans at the beginning of the nineteenth century. Knowledge created by historians is therefore ultimately relational, and the task of the historian is to deliver a comprehensive interpretation to her contemporary society and thus to provide meaning and orientation, a function which is characteristic of the humanities as a whole. And yet, the subjective dimension inadvertently contained in historical writing does not impair objectivity. The guarantee of this objectivity – for historians as well as for literature researchers – is method. Alongside the development of the discipline of history, several methods have been established: the historical-critical method of the German tradition following Schleiermacher or books like *The Historian's Craft* (Marc Bloch)[5] and *What Is History?* (E.H. Carr)[6] describe the methodological rules, sources and models against which the resulting narrative can be tested – and if it is in discord with them, such a narrative can be refuted as being a distorted image of the past. The chosen method thus restrains the multitude of interpretations by what can be found in the sources, and the method itself, its prescriptions and the models established by it remain non-arbitrary. As such, it guarantees verifiability and the intersubjective validity of the historical narrative. If this was not the case, erroneous and misleading interpretations of the past – take the works of holocaust deniers as an example – could not be refuted. By applying a rigorous method, historians can check which models stand the scrutiny of the sources and in this way ensure transparency about the processing of historical narratives. The objectivity of the narrative – be it in history or literature studies – is thus warranted by its embedding in science as a social system. It's also about the nature of knowledge – tolerance for ambiguity and uncertainty can be higher in a system based on 'preponderance of evidence' (careful interpretation) than on 'beyond a reasonable doubt' (proof of fact). Hence refuting conspiracy theories isn't necessarily effective for those determined to believe those elements of them that could be true.

Digitization and the change of interpretive practices in the humanities

With the beginning of the twenty-first century and the advent of digitization, the practice of historians and literary scholars began to change profoundly, as long-established epistemic cultures began to come into contact with the very different requirements of data-centric research. In the twentieth century, access to sources and primary literature was limited by the necessity to physically access cultural heritage institutions like archives and libraries. Travel bursaries were needed to visit these institutions, to consult finding aids and catalogues and to consult with archivists and librarians in order to unlock the knowledge embodied by them. Digitization now implies what could be described in Foucauldian terms as an 'epistemic rupture':[7] a profound reorganization of the knowledge base and the ways in which relevant sources are collected, organized and narrativized. With more and more metadata such as archival descriptions and information in catalogues becoming available online, the access to pertinent sources is potentially broadened; at the same time, other sources become obfuscated where metadata are not yet available or never will be for reasons of privacy or lack of description. On the side of the researchers, rich information environments require them to develop new skills to reduce noise and enhance signal, thus necessitating knowledge of new techniques which are not part of the classical formation provided by these disciplines.

Digitization can be regarded as a disruptive force here, since it does not entail simply bringing the long-established finding aids and cataloguing procedures into digital form. Rather, this information has to be brought into new formats according to metadata standards ensuring data exchange between institutions, interoperability, aggregation and scaling. The creation of metadata, a kind of description that seeks to organize knowledge rather than merely annotate and let the algorithm find patterns, is therefore crucial for the representation of complex knowledge, since it represents a shift in the scope of re-contextualization and at the same time redefines the terrain of researchers' exploration. In order to avoid levelling differences and to bypass reductive and limiting metadata structures, the experts establishing those data have to anticipate which possible research roads the users will take, a human determination of signal versus noise not always applied by data-centric approaches. Archivists and librarians need to provide context within given metadata standards, thus deprioritizing some knowledge by dint of elevating other knowledge over it. With online accessible metadata, archival descriptions and catalogue formats become the new interface between researchers and cultural heritage institutions. This profound shift in their relationship produces a range of yet uncertain consequences: firstly, the aim of having all descriptions of available material online signals to users that the dialogic exchange with the archivists and librarians may be superfluous. For historians, this may result in bypassing the knowledge embodied in cultural heritage practitioners, as will be discussed in the next chapters. With users becoming enabled to explore the entirety of the cultural heritage collections online, their terrain of discovery becomes enlarged, and the archivists' scope of re-contextualization gets reduced. Cultural heritage practitioners themselves notice their own detachment from knowledge they presided over. Thus the power structures regarding access to knowledge and knowledge creation change. Furthermore, researchers struggle to acquire the competences necessary to perform complex searches. This presents a huge challenge since the most fruitful knowledge enquiries require an intimate knowledge about the specific data structures in which relevant information is presented, not just familiarity with relevant keywords. For historians, their formative training provided the skills necessary to navigate through finding aids and the traditional hierarchical structure of archival collections through which contextual connections could be traced. Keyword searches may act as an approximation, with important consequences for the complexity of the search results, especially with regard to archival sources that may not be captured by this kind of approach.

For literary scholars, digitization of primary material free of copyright provided access to broad corpora; hundreds of thousands of books were now available in digital format, endowed with machine and human readable transcriptions via optical character recognition (OCR). While Computational Literary Criticism had been confined to a manageable number of texts and had focused on authorship attribution until the 1980s, the availability of large corpora required the application of statistical methods. This shift in the paradigm of knowledge production was not welcomed by every part of the community of philologists.[8] The need to establish filtering procedures to pick a manageable corpus of texts relevant for the research question brought the interplay between individual researchers, their research environments and the libraries and infrastructures providing metadata to the fore, and decisions on the tools and methods appropriate for the available research objects had to be reflected carefully upon. It is not by chance that text-oriented digital humanists took up classical knowledge discovery instruments like indices and registers known from book printing. This observation can be substantiated with regard to the enthusiasm of the digital humanities for subject, topic and person indexes and directories of places, which correspond to techniques such as topic modelling or named entity recognition (NER), or their preference for visualizations such as maps and chronologies or timelines. All these examples refer to classification and categorization systems as have always been contained in historical books, and which preform insight and knowledge. Moreover, the context-dependency of data introduces the suspicion that they might not render it possible to determine the meaning. As one of the KPLEX interviewees from a computer science background stated:

> If I read this and then I read this one, I cannot say which one is correct because it's like it depends on the context and I am not in this context. So it's really hard to it's like once you get the data and you remove the context, you don't know any more what – maybe there are hidden parameters and you don't know them, there are hidden variables that, you know, condition the way data have been collected, and once you don't know any more what these variable are it's very hard to describe.
>
> (WP2 INT2)

New techniques like data cleaning had to be acquired by philologists who were accustomed to a strong reverence for the printed word. Data cleaning does not only imply the correction of OCR errors, but also the processing of texts by removing stopwords, calculating term frequencies, identifying the most frequent bi- and trigrams and so on. These techniques are apt for substituting distant reading where close reading is the norm, but at the same time those readers accustomed to interpret the polysemy and ambiguity of words and phrases immediately identified data cleaning as a procedure which obfuscates as much as it elaborates. The provision of metadata, for example, the indications of the literary genre recorded in a library catalogue, was questioned as a valid source of information, since they immediately become recognizable as time-bound social constructions.

The establishment of metadata as the new interfaces between researchers and their research material also has had consequences for the creation of narratives. Certainly, scholars are still required to directly access sources and primary material in the very same way as they did in the twentieth century. But with the shift to digital discoverability and the establishment of newly created metadata as the primary point of entry, metadata occupy a new role. As the organizing scheme that facilitates accessibility and discoverability of data, they inevitably support and preform the transformation of data into narratives. In this manner, metadata become a sort of actor, shaping and reshaping the range of possible narratives that can be created.[9] It is hard to predict the consequences this has for scholars and the narratives they produce, and even more difficult to estimate the outcomes of this Foucauldian power shift in knowledge creation for the insights and narratives gained through the analysis of big data aggregated on the basis of these metadata.

The historical sciences and big data

It is remarkable to note the distance of historical science from the terms 'data' and 'big data', especially with regard to the observation that 'big data' – or at least their forerunner – have always been at the hands of historians. One may think of the nineteenth century, for example, where the economy was still predominantly agrarian and strong bureaucracies like the one in Prussia collected large amounts of historical records on agriculture and demography for statistical and fiscal purposes. The disinterest on the side of historians for these sources which can still be found in the archives, and the accompanying indifference to numbers, is therefore in need of an explanation. This can only be understood by a deep dive into the history of historiography, and here the story begins in Germany, which was, according to British Historian Blackbourn, 'not only the home of modern, archival, "scientific" history, but an international leader in philosophy, philology and law',[10] so while the trends we are looking at have general applicability, we can use the German historical frame as a point of reference for their origins.

One of the important pioneers of German historicism was Johann Gottfried Herder, who reaccentuated the interpretation of the past and brought the conception of 'Volk' as an agent to the connection between period and culture.[11] The German 'Volk' as a subject of history, from which cultural and societal conditions silently emerge: it was this master narrative which forms Herder's lasting contribution to historiography. Furthermore, before the establishment of the discipline, Wilhelm von Humboldt's reflections on how scientific knowledge of past realities can be created by contemporaries and how understanding is possible at all paved the way for a theory of historical hermeneutics as well as the development of the historical-critical method. Finally, as a third important source, enlightenment's philosophy of history has to be named, especially with respect to romantic conceptions of the 'Volk' as the source of language and customs, of law and poetry, and Hegel's concept of history as having a direction and a telos, as progress towards freedom.

Nourished by these sources, classical philology yielded classical and ancient studies, and developed in Germany throughout the nineteenth century into historical science. German historical scholarship gained an extraordinary prestige, especially with regard to historical encyclopaedias. Moreover, also jurisprudence developed into a historical science, with leading figures such as Karl von Savigny and Karl Friedrich Eichhorn. With historicism taking hold, Niebuhr and especially Leopold von Ranke transformed historiography into a strict science. Ranke performed a recalibration of the focus of historiography on politics, government, constitution, law, churches and institutions. With this shift, the emphasis of historical science went over from culture and 'Volk' to the nation state. In this way, historical science and historiography became between 1840 and 1870 a politically oriented, engaged science dealing with the identity of the citizens of a nation, with freedom and emancipation, progress and political unity. German unification in 1871 then provided a boost for nationalist historians like Sybel, Droysen and Treitschke; at the same time, the prospering economy and the advantages of the German Reich – such as the harmonization of currency and patents, the rule of law and a liberal commercial code – were welcomed by the liberals.[12] A common notion of progress undergirded the establishment of the paradigm of modernization. It is not surprising that contemporaries were obsessed with statistics to show how everything was becoming larger, better or quicker. The German railway became a symbol of progress, as became everything connected to steam-power – steam engines, steam ploughs and steamboats. Beyond this fixation on technical modernization and material improvement, social and cultural advance became a testimony to German progress, and the national historiography of the German late nineteenth century concentrated these elements into a narrative creating a sense of identification. With its focus on the nation-state and the triumphant representation of the German Reich as the telos of history, historical science took a central position within the sciences and the humanities remained among them as a 'Wissenschaft' then and to this day. While this process took place in Germany during the phase of the differentiation of the scientific disciplines in the nineteenth century, at the same time classical national economy and the theory of the liberal-capitalistic economic system were developed mainly in Great Britain (Adam Smith, David Ricardo). In contrast to this upsurge, hardly little more than the reception of these advances can be noted in Germany. It is therefore not surprising that almost no integration into the historical sciences took place there, which can best be seen from the disregard German historians had (and still have) for Karl Marx and his theory. German national economy developed a focus on the social question and on a rather sociologically oriented empirical-statistical social research. If data on economy, on social classes and social stratum as well as on behaviour make up what we would now call 'big data', it is obvious that the establishment and consolidation of disciplines like macroeconomics, statistics, sociology and psychology – and the collection of the respective data – have taken place alongside with the formation of the specific functions of historical science and its neglect of numerical data in the late nineteenth century. Furthermore, in contrast to the occupation of the historians working in archives and being concerned with primary sources, these disciplines are marked by a strong division of labour, with longer chains from the data collector up to the scientist compared to how historians work. While macroeconomics, statistics, sociology and psychology may therefore be much more acquainted to the term 'data', it has to be noted that their process of knowledge production is marked by an alienation from the sources in a more profound way than in the historical sciences.

Numbers and description, narrative and interpretation

In order to explain the distance of the historical and literary sciences from the term 'data' and to characterize the way in which these disciplines make sense out of the primary material, one has to look at the yet under-researched question of the epistemological relationship between numbers and interpretation. Here it is noteworthy that etymology points to the common roots of the terms 'to count' and 'to re-count',[13] of 'to tally' and 'to tell'[14] or, in German, of 'zählen' and 'erzählen'.[15] The historical meaning of these words therefore refers to the relationship between description and interpretation, between enumeration and storytelling. 'Counting' may have been used here, in a pre-modern and pre-scientific context, in a self-referential, tautological way to count the most obvious (such as fingers, people, oxen). Understood in this way, it points to objectively independent entities which cannot be modified at will. This brings us back to the concerns of the last chapter, as what is counted therefore meets the definition of 'datum', a 'given' which cannot be changed. At the same time this very fundamental understanding meets the definition of 'fact', insofar as it can be proven to be true with evidence and is independent of opinion and interpretation. 'Re-counting', in its pre-modern meaning, simply designates telling a story or constructing an account of that which has been counted and which has been ordered (first this, then that and so on), in the sense of narratively going along a sequence of numbers. It is here where Mary Poovey has mounted her *History of the Modern Fact*, by which she narrates how two functions – describing and interpreting – came to seem separate from each other in the early modern period, and how numbers, condensed in figures, came to seem distinct from interpretation. In analysing historical debates about induction and by studying authors such as Adam Smith, Thomas Malthus and William Petty, she comes to the following conclusion: 'Separating numbers from interpretive narrative, that is, reinforced the assumption that numbers were different in kind from the analytic accounts that accompanied them.'[16] Poovey is able to show that in the pre-history of 'the modern fact' two dimensions became intertwined: first of all, the assumption about epistemology that systematic knowledge should be derived from (and as such is superior to) non-interpretive descriptions. Numbers and quantities were seen as a disinterested representation of objectively verifiable units. Figures, therefore, simultaneously seem to describe discrete particulars, represent quantified items and serve analytic accounts, and thus seemed to be different in representational kinds. According to Poovey, the second dimension dates back to the seventeenth century, where members of the British Royal Society discussed arguments about the possibility to collect data immune from theory or interpretation and thus opened a gap between theory-free particulars and systematic knowledge. Such a separation of observation from systematic account, inherited from the early modern period, severs the connection between description and interpretation and implies the non-interpretive, value-free and ontologically different status of numbers. Even though it can be read from nineteenth-century texts that even numbers were understood to be interpretive because every quantification embodies theoretical assumptions of what should be counted, by that time two modes of representation had become customarily graphically separated: numbers (presented in figures) and text (forming the narrative commentary).

The relationship between description and interpretation within the larger frame of the epistemological process changed with the reconfiguration of the conception of objectivity in the late nineteenth and early twentieth century and the emergence of mechanical objectivity.[17] As Daston and Galison explain in their book, objectivity and subjectivity are inextricably bound together, with objectivity meaning the suppression of some aspects of the subject as well as the artificial division of the researcher-subject into an active experimenter and a passive observer. In the nineteenth century, scientists developed an ethos obliging researchers to restrain themselves in order to repress their wilful intervention and acquire virtues like patience, tirelessness and industriousness; furthermore, procedures were developed in order to reliably bring observations from nature onto the page documenting the scientist's activities through a strict protocol. The development of photography is emblematic in this emergence of mechanical objectivity, and two intertwined processes are at work here: On the one hand, the separation of the development and activities of machines from the human beings who conceived of them, with the result that machines were attributed freedom from the wilful interventions that had come to be seen as the most dangerous aspects of subjectivity. Thus machines – be they cameras, sensors or electronic devices, or indeed the data they produce – have become emblematic for the elimination of human agency and embody objectivity without subjectivity. On the other hand, the ideal of mechanical objectivity also implied alterations on the side of the subject of the researcher, favouring non-intervention and evolving around practices including 'training the senses in scientific observation, keeping lab notebooks, drawing specimens, habitually monitoring one's own beliefs and hypotheses, quieting the will, and channelling the attention'.[18] Thus an ethics of objectivity was developed, which called for a morality of self-restraint in order to hold researchers back from intervention and interferences like overinterpretation, aestheticization and theoretical overreaching, precisely the kinds of hesitations around narrative we see in the KPLEX interview cited earlier in this chapter. The emergence of mechanical objectivity thus also reconfigured the relationship between description and interpretation: while photography became emblematic for objective truth, self-elimination in the interpretation of automatically transferred records became a precept for the scientists. Even though contemporary researchers may have been fully aware of an epistemology comprising the design and construction of machines for the purpose of data collection according to given research questions, the persistence of the belief that machines deliver impartial and objective records of a reality is remarkable and can only be explained with the auratization of mechanically fabricated products like photographs. At the same time it is obvious that such a conception of a division between a mechanical device responsible for collecting and recording data and the researcher responsible for impartially making sense of what had been collected is disjunct from the activities of historians and literature researchers who are occupied with the interpretation of sources and research material produced and collected prior to the beginning of their research. This is not to say that historians do not use mechanically produced materials like photographs for their studies or that they did not adhere to virtues like self-discipline, self-restraint and self-control. Methodologies like the critical assessment of the sources have been developed as technologies to control and curtail the dangers contained in the judgements of the researchers. But historians have simply not invented mechanical devices to collect the information that they need for answering their research questions. In this way, the term 'data' has become alien and unusual to historians – and to humanists in general – and data do not form the primary source out of which interpretation and narratives are created.

Science as a social system: The social construction of meaning

While the development of mechanical objectivity can be seen as decisive in setting the course for the epistemic bifurcation between the natural sciences and the humanities, there is still the need to explain why common sense still attributes objectivity and impartiality to data and identifies them with facts, whilst interpretation and narrative are seen as being ontologically distinct from them. This has to do with the different social systems and the peculiarities and customs that have emerged in the various scientific disciplines. As has been noted above, for historians and literature scholars, the establishment of models, the strict application of methods, the reference to sources to enable transparency, and the questioning and discussion of the research results by the audience of peers are basic elements by which the objectivity of the scientific narrative is guaranteed. These agonistic disputes seem to function well as an internal corrective, even though the case of the German 'Historikerstreit' shows that such a debate may remain unresolved. Generally speaking, scientific knowledge is socially constructed because it is partly derived from collective beliefs held by scientific communities.[19] Beyond the activity of the individual researcher, the embedding of research results within a broader scientific discourse shows that scientific research is a collective activity. Each scientific collective develops characteristic habits and customs of directed perception which shapes the ways in which the members of the collective perceive and think about the world, and which is responsible for a shared understanding of what is accepted as evidence.[20] Daston and Galison call this 'trained judgement'.[21] Acquired habits are also responsible for the community of researchers to 'forget' that an object has been declared a scientific fact by virtue of convention and learning. Although researchers are aware of the acquisition of these abilities, they accept it as tacit knowledge. Learning to see like a scientist is a question of accumulated experience. Collectives of scientists therefore develop and learn as part of their professional formation, and the acceptance and recognition within the scientific collective form an important precondition for the approval or dismissal of the hypotheses brought forward in scientific studies within the larger scientific discourse in which they are debated. Much of what is termed 'science' therefore relies on social practices and procedures of adjudication. As the historian of science Naomi Oreskes has recently commented, the heterogeneity of the scientific community supports the strength of the achieved consensus: 'Objectivity is likely to be maximized when [...] the community is sufficiently diverse that a broad range of views can be developed, heard, and appropriately considered.'[22] Ultimately, the processes performed within such scientific communities result in what is designated as 'truth'.

While the quality of such consensual scientific knowledge may depend on factors like the level of abstraction and complexity, the agreement on the appropriate methods to answer the debated questions, or the ideological orientation of the participants, the reliance on sources which have not been created and collected according to certain research questions remains as a feature distinguishing these humanistic disciplines from natural sciences like biology. In the latter disciplines, the design and development of devices and laboratories constructed to assume the task of data collection assumed an enormous extent in the twentieth century and involved significant material investments. Data were now created in abundance, and an important feature of scientific discovery consisted in the use of procedures to create an account out of the chaos of available perceptions, that is, creating order out of disorder by making sense of the observations at hand. In their pioneering study entitled *Laboratory Life*, Latour and Woolgar analysed what they described as the social construction of scientific knowledge and as the process of establishment and enforcement of statements and data as 'facts'.[23] Social constructivism, the sociological theory which forms the background of the study, focuses on the social situatedness of knowledge construction through human interaction. It is precisely this situatedness which allows the process of fact construction to be described as one in which social factors disappear and the traces of their constructedness become difficult to detect. This does not imply that facts are entirely constructed, because then they would be artefacts; in what has now become a famous paradoxical formula, Latour and Woolgar describe the way 'in which the term fact can simultaneously mean what is fabricated and what is not fabricated':[24] On the one hand, they point to the etymology of the word 'fact' as derived from the Latin terms 'facere' and 'factum' (to make or to do) and underline the process of its construction; on the other hand, they explain that scientific statements 'are referred to as a thing "out there" (objectivity and fact)'.[25] In other words, what is termed 'fact' can certainly be found in and verified by the collected data, but at the same time it is subject to a process of purification from social factors. Science appears here as a negotiation process in an agonistic arena, in which some forces bring forward statements which prove the artefact-like status by proving social involvement (subjectivity) in the process, while other forces push statements forward which speak for the fact-like status or the 'out-there-ness' (objectivity). The whole process ensures that once the debate settles facts are taken for granted. The paradoxical nature of 'facts' therefore reflects the process of data production by assertedly neutral and impartial machines which have been designed by humans according to specific research interests and which therefore rather deliver 'capta' than 'data', and the scientific – and therefore inevitably social – activities around the construction of facts and their recognition as such by a scientific collective.

The larger part of Latour and Woolgar's study is devoted to the analysis of the process of social construction and describes the long line from the construction of facts, the result of which is that facts appear not to be constructed by anyone, up to the presentation of a credible account which aims at affirming and defending the existence of those facts in the arena formed by the collective of scientists. Other than simplistic conceptions of a binary relationship between data/ facts (or description/observation) and accounts (or interpretation/narrative), Latour and Woolgar describe the construction of facts as a complex process of negotiations which includes moving back and forth between the two poles. This process includes the elimination of alternative interpretations of scientific data and the rendering of these alternatives as less plausible (e.g. by delegitimising interpretations brought forward by rivalling scientists), the vanishing of elements which are described as circumstances from the final accounts, the introduction of inequality into a set of equally probable statements in such a way that a statement is taken to be more probable than all the alternatives (a technique to decrease noise in the data), the increase of cost for others to raise equally probable alternatives which results out of the material provisions with which the laboratory is equipped (the operationalization of economic capital), the credibility (or accumulated symbolic capital) of the scientist which supports her accreditation and creates the credit needed for holding her account accountable and, as a final activity, the writing and publication of scientific articles, which form a central activity of creating order and a socially accepted reality. While the study by Latour and Woolgar is restricted to the specific research setting of a laboratory, it is fascinating to see how rare studies of this kind are, and to perceive the lack of profound observation of scientific practices in general. Certainly, this is one of the reasons why the collection, analysis and interpretation of big data are shrouded in mystery, especially when it comes to the analysis of the complex chains from data to interpretation in the inaccessible towers of knowledge production erected by large tech companies.

Making sense of big data

Latour and Woolgar analysed a setting in which data were produced in abundance. The social construction of facts includes various procedures enabling the discrimination of signal and noise; the researchers in the laboratory inspect large datasets conflated in tables and graphs. This situation has intensified considerably with the rise of big data. These are per se data which have been collected by machines and are too big to be inspected by humans. Their magnitude has consequences: they are so large that typical applications to store, compute and analyse them are inappropriate. Often processing them is a challenge for a single computer; thus, a cluster of computers has to be used in parallel. Or the amount of data has to be reduced by mapping an unstructured dataset to a dataset where individual elements are key-value pairs; on a reduced selection of these key-value pairs mathematical analyses can be performed ('MapReduce'). Even though big data are often not collected in response to a specific research question, their sheer size (millions of observations x of variables y) promises to provide answers relevant for a large part of a society's population, as will be discussed more broadly in Chapter 7. From a statistical point of view, what happens is that large sample sizes boost significance; the effect size is more important. However, on the other hand, large does not mean all; one has to be aware of the universe covered by the data. Statistical inference – conclusions drawn from data about the population as a whole – cannot easily be applied, because the datasets are not established in a way that ensures that they are representative.[26] Beyond parallel computing and MapReduce, the use of machine learning seems to provide viable solutions to handle big data. Machine learning designates algorithms that can learn from and make predictions on data by building a model from sample inputs. It is a type of artificial intelligence in which the system learns from lots of examples; results – such as patterns or clusters – become stronger with more evidence. It is for this reason why big data and machine learning seem to go hand in hand. Machine learning can roughly be divided into two approaches: on the one hand, analytic techniques which use stochastic data models, most often classification and regression in supervised learning and, on the other hand, predictive approaches, where the data mechanism is unknown, as it is the case with neural nets and deep learning.

The goal of statistical modelling is to find a model which allows quantitative conclusions to be drawn from data. It has the advantage of the data model being transparent and comprehensible to the analyst. Statisticians in applied research consider data modelling as the template for statistical analysis and focus within their range of multivariate analysis tools on discriminant analysis and logistic regression in classification, and multiple linear regression in regression. This approach has the advantage that it produces a simple and understandable picture of the relationship between the input variables and response. But the assumption that the data model is an emulation of nature is not necessarily valid and can lead to wrong conclusions. What sounds objective since it is 'based on statistics' is not necessarily correct as, if the model is a poor emulation of reality, the conclusions may be wrong. This is the reason Cathy O'Neill has called an algorithm 'an opinion formalized in code'[27] – it does not simply provide objectivity, but works towards the goals for which it was written.

In recent years, powerful new tools for big data analysis have been developed: neural nets and deep learning algorithms. The goal of these tools is predictive accuracy; they are hardware hungry and data hungry, but have their strength in addressing complex prediction problems where it is obvious that stochastic data models are not applicable. Therefore, the approach is designed in another way here: what is observed is a set of x's that go in and a subsequent set of y's that come out. The challenge is to find an algorithm such that for future x in a test set, the result of that algorithm being applied to x will be a good predictor of y. The goal is to have the algorithm produce results with a strong predictive accuracy. The focus does not lie with the model by which the input x is transformed into the output y; it does not have to be a stochastic data model. Rather, the model is unknown, complex, mysterious and irrelevant. This is the reason why accurate prediction methods are addressed as complex 'black boxes'. As opposed to the case with stochastic models, the goal is not interpretability, but accurate information. And it is here on the basis of an opaque data model, where neural nets and deep learning extract features from big data and identify patterns or clusters which have been invisible to the human analyst. It is fascinating to see that humans don't decide or predetermine what those features are. The predictive analysis of big data can identify and magnify patterns hidden in the data.

The interpretation of the results of big data analyses therefore implies a choice between the devil and the deep blue sea: either the analyst may rely on a data model that is comprehensible to her, in full awareness of the deficiencies of such a model, since the complexity of the world far outstrips the stochastic data models which have been constructed to explain it ('all models are wrong'[28]), or the analyst resigns herself to the 'black box' and the high predictive power associated with it, being fully aware that correlation is not equivalent to causation, resulting in the separation of understanding and knowledge. With the availability of a growing amount of big data, computational power and the work of capable developers of algorithms, the approach based on stochastic data models has become outdated in favour of predictive accuracy. But the lack of interpretability of the relationship between prediction and response variables accompanying the latter approach widens the gap between understanding and knowledge and renders narratives dysfunctional, since they rely on the power to explain causal relationships. Scientific narratives have always carved out such relationships in multiple ways and are therefore key to human understanding of the complex world around them. With the advance of big data and AI, central elements of scientific understanding – like principles, laws, models, generalizations and representativeness – lose their worth. Such a development leads to structural blindness: since it is still humans who make decisions on the basis of their interpretations of data, they are deprived of key tools used in the interpretive process, which enable the generation and collateralization of narratives, discussion of uncertainties and doubts, and ensure the adherence to methodological rules and models against which the results can be tested. As a consequence, Law Professor Frank Pasquale has warned that 'authority is increasingly expressed algorithmically. Decisions that used to be based on human reflection are now made automatically.'[29] Finally, the analysis of big data and the application of artificial intelligence in specialized laboratories owned by private corporations entail that the researchers working there are being cut off from the obligation to have their research results discussed and approved by relevant scientific communities, as it is the case with state-funded researchers who have to justify why they should be funded.

While it has become obvious that big data inherit the aura of data and facts as disinterested representations ensuring objectivity, it is often overlooked that big data have their specificities as well: as scalable data, they view individuals as representatives of social groups, identify subjects as 'users' or 'customers' rather than as citizens or members of a community (yet more revealing linguistic habits of technology firms, such as were discussed in the last chapter), focus on consumption patterns rather than the significance and meaning attributed to them by the individual and take behaviour into perspective instead of the inner life.[30] Human beings are not perceived as individuals in a holistic way, but in their partial existence as producers of data or money. Out of this homogenizing force results an indifference towards meaningful particularities of a given world, an insensitivity towards cultural differences and an incapacity for the evaluation of uncertain, hazardous and conflicting information. Finally, the inability to incorporate knowledge which is not scalable – like context – impairs the development of a profound understanding of the particular. Against this backdrop it is necessary to underline that the humanities not only involve a different way of creating meaning entailing the critical assessment of sources, the representation of non linearity in developments, reflections of the method, an openness to double-checking and rivalling interpretations, the discussion of alternative approaches and research results, and the inclusion of thick description and context to ensure narrative richness, but also that the function of the narratives delivered by them is quite distinct from those of interpretations of big data: the provision of identities, of orientation and societally relevant sensemaking, and a critical reflection of the past for the present and the future.

Notes

1 Warburg Institute, *Lorraine Daston: Exempla and the Epistemology of the Humanities*, 2016, https://www.youtube.com/watch?v=8JlXfIyqsG4.

2 Von Ranke, Leopold, 'Geschichten der romanischen und germanischen Völker von 1494 bis 1514', in *Leopold von Ranke's Sämmtliche Werke*, 2nd edn (Leipzig: Duncker und Humblot, 1874), 33/34, VII.

3 This can be read, for example, from Ranke's statement which reveals – through the use of the irrealis – his consciousness about a remaining rest of subjectivity: 'Ich wünschte mein Selbst gleichsam auszulöschen, und nur die Dinge reden, die mächtigen Kräfte erscheinen zu lassen.' Von Ranke, Leopold, 'Englische Geschichte vornehmlich im siebzehnten Jahrhundert', in *Leopold von Ranke's Sämmtliche Werke*, 3rd edn (Leipzig: Duncker und Humblot, 1870), 15.2, 103.

4 Nipperdey, Thomas, *Deutsche Geschichte 1800–1866: Bürgerwelt und starker Staat*, 5th edn (Munich: C.H. Beck, 1991), 12.

5 Bloch, Marc, *The Historian's Craft* (New York: Knopf, 1953).

6 Carr, Edward Hallet, *What Is History?* (London: Macmillan, 1961).

7 Foucault, Michel, *The Order of Things: An Archaeology of the Human Sciences* (New York: Pantheon Books, 1970).

8 A valuable and concise history of Computational Literary Criticism is provided by Beausang, Chris, 'A Brief History of the Theory and Practice of Computational Literary Criticism (1963–2020)', *Magazén*, 2, 2020, JournalArticle_4061.

9 Edmond, Jennifer and Georgina Nugent Folan, 'Data, Metadata, Narrative. Barriers to the Reuse of Cultural Sources', in *Metadata and Semantic Research*, ed. Emmanouel Garoufallou, Sirje Virkus, Rania Siatri and Damiana Koutsomiha, Communications in Computer and Information Science (Cham: Springer, 2017), 253–60.

10 Blackbourn, David, *History of Germany 1780–1918: The Long Nineteenth Century* (Malden, MA: Blackwell, 2005), 208.

11 Nipperdey, *Deutsche Geschichte 1800–1866*, 498–533; Herder, Johann Gottfried and Michael N Forster, *Philosophical Writings* (Cambridge, UK: Cambridge University Press, 2002); Barnard, Frederick M, *Herder's Social and Political Thought* (Oxford: Clarendon Press, 1967).

12 Blackbourn, *History of Germany 1780–1918: The Long Nineteenth Century*, 204–14.

13 'Count [ME]: The verb to count is from Latin *computare* "to calculate", the root also of Computer, account [ME], and recount [LME] "tell" (which can also be used for

both "narrate" and "count")'. Cresswell, Julia, *Oxford Dictionary of Word Origins*, 2nd edn (Oxford: Oxford University Press, 2010), 104.

14 'To Tell, [Taellan or Tylean, Sax. Teler, Du. Zaehlen, Teut.] to count or number. To Tell, [Tellan, Tax. Talen, Du. Tale, Dan.] to relate, to make known.' Bailey, Nathan, *An Universal Etymological English Dictionary* (Hildesheim/NewYork: Georg Olms Verlag, 1721).

15 'erzählen *Vsw std.* (8.Jh.) mhd. *erzeln, erzellen*, ahd. *irzellen*. Bedeutet ursprünglich ‚aufzählen', dann, in geordneter Folge hersagen, berichten', woraus durch Verallgemeinerung die heutige Bedeutung entstand. Abstraktum: Erzählung; Nomen Agentis: Erzähler.' – 'zählen *Vsw std.* (8.Jh.) mhd. *zel(e)n, zellen*, ahd. *zellen*, as. *tellian.* Ae. *tellan*, anord. *telja* aus g. *tal-ija-* ‚zählen'. Ableitung von Zahl. 'Präfigierung: erzählen; Abstraktum: Zählung'. Kluge, Friedrich, *Etymologisches Wörterbuch der deutschen Sprache*, 25th edn (Berlin/Boston: De Gruyter, 2011), 258, 1000.

16 Poovey, Mary, *A History of the Modern Fact: Problems of Knowledge in the Sciences of Wealth and Society* (Chicago: University of Chicago Press, 1998), xv.

17 Daston, Lorraine J and Peter Louis Galison, *Objectivity* (New York: Zone Books, 2015), 115–90.

18 Ibid., 199.

19 Fleck, Ludwig, *Genesis and Development of a Scientific Fact* (Chicago: Chicago University Press, 1979).

20 And this disciplinarity is then inscribed on the data themselves – data are constituted as belonging to one discipline and not another, in a linguistic sense of their not being understandable by other disciplines but also in that they are playing a role in defining that discipline in a Bernstein(ean) sense, as discussed in Chapter 2.

21 Datson and Galison, *Objectivity*, 370–1.

22 Oreskes, Naomi, *Why Trust Science?* (Princeton: Princeton University Press, 2019), 53.

23 Latour, Bruno and Steve Woolgar, *Laboratory Life: The Social Construction of Scientific Facts, Beverly Hills* (Beverly Hills/London: Sage Publications, 1979).

24 Ibid., 236.

25 Ibid.,180.

26 Kitchin, Rob, *The Data Revolution: Big Data, Open Data, Data Infrastructures and Their Consequences* (London: Sage), 19.

27 O'Neil, Cathy, *Weapons of Math Destruction: How Big Data Increases Inequality and Threatens Democracy* (New York: Crown, 2016), 53.

28 So, Richard, Jean, "'All Models Are Wrong'", *PMLA*, 132/3 (2017), 668–73.

29 Pasquale, Frank A, *The Black Box Society: The Secret Algorithms That Control Money and Information* (Cambridge, MA: Harvard University Press, 2015), 8.

30 Madsbjerg, Christian, *Sensemaking: What Makes Human Intelligence Essential in the Age of the Algorithm* (London: Little, Brown, 2017), 199–211.

4

Please mind the gap: The problems of information voids in the knowledge discovery process

We have outsourced our memory to online search engines, in particular Google, and just search for the 'fact' we cannot remember. Even the proprietary name Google, now one of the world's biggest technology companies,[1,2] has transmogrified into a verb: 'Why don't you google it?' Web search engines have become embedded into our daily lives; we view information and knowledge through the lens of a search engine, generating a one-dimensional list-map of the knowledge landscape related to the keyword search query we have served to a ranking algorithm parsing a powerful, but by no means exhaustive, index of information sources. In over 70 per cent of cases,[3,4] our process of seeking an information source is satisficed[5] within the first page of results; however, for complex, culturally entangled research questions the most significant sources in the knowledge landscape are rarely near the top of the ranked query results. Not all research resources are accessible through search queries and even knowledge of their existence may not be available to the search engine user.

In many research disciplines where there exist well-known big data datasets which have been collaboratively created or are the output of sensors or other devices, there is little need to use search engines or AI agents for data discovery. However, in disciplines such as the humanities and the social sciences[6] research data may come from disparate sources often held by more than one cultural heritage institution (CHI), accompanied by the kinds of rich contextual flows discussed in Chapter 2.

In this chapter we will discuss the challenges of gaps in the knowledge creation process caused by the process of locating research resources within the human record through search engines and how this is reshaping the response of the traditional keepers of cultural heritage data to the changing ways in which their communities of researchers wish to interact.

The dominance of search engines

The strength of the World Wide Web (Web) is in the hyperlink. It seems obvious now, as we can spend an inordinate amount of our time 'clicking' links in the hope that the next Web page of information delivered to our screen is the one that really answers the question we have. The Web's success lies in its ability to satisfy with little risk,[7] but does it do this, or do we spend too much time searching for a specific nugget of knowledge? More specifically, can a researcher investigating a complex cultural or historical issue actually find a specific piece of information or dataset held in a CHI before, or even without, turning up at their door? And, if she can find it, can she use it? Is its context clear? Is it complete, or its gaps visible? Is it in a language the researcher can read?

Tim Berners-Lee, in his CERN paper of 1989 'Information Management: A Proposal' suggested that CERN could benefit from 'a web of notes with links (like references) between them is far more useful than a fixed hierarchical system'.[8] Indeed, since many researchers at CERN were on secondment, bound to return to their home institutions, a web of notes accessible from anywhere was what was needed to maintain research activities, and was what Berners-Lee & Robert Cailliau developed.

> HyperText is a way to link and access information of various kinds as a web of nodes in which the user can browse at will. ... There is a potential large benefit from the integration of a variety of systems in a way which allows a user to follow links pointing from one piece of information to another one.[9]

Ted Nelson introduced the term 'hypertext' to express a corpus of 'written or pictorial material' which could not be 'presented or represented on paper' due to its complexity of interconnections. Furthermore, the hypertext may include summaries and maps of its content, and like any scholarly text it may have the addition of annotations and footnotes by scholars.[10]

> Its purpose was to create techniques for handling personal file systems and manuscripts in progress. These two purposes are closely related and not sharply distinct. Many writers and research professionals have files or collections of notes which are tied to manuscripts in progress. Indeed, often personal files shade into manuscripts, and the assembly of textual notes becomes the writing of text without a sharp break.[11]

We are only now approaching Nelson's vision for scholarly communication,[12] via Berners-Lee & Cailliau's World Wide Web, with the first examples of hypertext annotation services and research infrastructures that facilitate the discovery, gathering and management of research resources. As can be observed with the Semantic Web,[13] where information is more useful if it is expressly linked to other information, associating new knowledge with existing knowledge in a data infrastructure may present researchers with a transformative tool rather than the paginated metaphor of the Web.

The linking of snippets of knowledge, or as semantic assertions[14] via a browsable (knowledge) graph,[15] to form insight, understanding and new knowledge, can have both advantages (trust through association) and disadvantages (incorrect assertions). We see this data linking value occur in scholarly activities such as the use of nanopublications,[16] and not-for-profit activities such as Wikidata[17] and GeoNames.[18]

As the Web grew rapidly with so much information to discover and digest, all users faced information overload.[19] Browsing presented little risk but cost in terms of time spent in fruitless foraging. However, browsing led to the discovery of serendipitous knowledge, and potentially more time wasted. In an environment of favourite site listings and printed directories,[20] search engines with large databases of keyworded URLs emerged as a method to attempt to organize knowledge through curated interfaces such as that of Yahoo! at the time. The need to access information accurately and quickly led to the rise of the Web search engine[21] and in particular Google in 1998.[22] At this time browsing the Web was as important as searching. Then, Google changed everything. The Google homepage still looks similar today as it always has; however, it was how Google collected its index and the page-ranking algorithm that made it the preeminent search engine and the *de facto* way we locate and access Web resources, eclipsing the variety and potentially diverse strengths of the kinds of approaches common to specialists in cultural heritage.

Ranking and the long tail problem

What makes Google different can, in part, be attributed to its PageRank algorithm[23] which ranked Web pages by an objective measure of link importance utilizing the topology of the interconnection of hyperlinks to calculate the ranking, relevance or quality of each Web page,[24] or authority in the graph of links created by PageSearch.[25] Unlike other search engines, at the time of Google's launch, it was able to produce search result lists with the most relevant and useful Web pages at the top.[26] Web users could still encounter problems in finding relevant information since when a simple keyword query is entered and the resultant list of Web pages are ranked on their similarity to the keywords[27] which may not be well chosen. Kosala and Blockeel considered that there was a problem of low precision resulting from the irrelevance of many of the search results. Such low precision is part of the so-called long-tail problem of search queries where, for any general query, the majority of resultant Web page references listed have low rankings due to few interconnecting inbound hyperlinks. This is a phenomenon that is well known and a particular challenge for complex cultural research questions, when the research resources of interest are likely to be referenced uniquely (thus lowly ranked by PageRank) amongst tens or even hundreds of thousands of possible results listed. In 2012 Google started to roll out the use of a knowledge graph to aid the recognition of, and the discovery of, real world entities.[28] This knowledge graph is visually presented as a side panel with associated details about the entity and suggestions for browsing similar entities in the form of 'People also search for' links. However, the knowledge graph does not appear to provide additional information for entities which do not have an entry in a key resource such as Wikipedia or Google Books. Thus, even with accessing the Google knowledge graph, the vast wealth of results is overwhelming in terms of numbers but not quality. Even with refining a search query using the Google common search techniques,[29] a researcher is still required to hunt through considerable quantities of resultant Web pages.

Equally, for CHIs holding resources of relevance to scholars, it is difficult to promote their holdings via the likes of Google even if they have expertise in search engine optimization (SEO), which is examined further in Chapter 6. Academic researchers are not necessarily the largest demographic of users for all CHIs, though they are a community which take up a significant proportion of time for the institution's staff.[30] How an institution manages its migration to an external digital representation and communications is perhaps one of their biggest challenges currently. The browse metaphor[31] may prove to be a better discovery strategy for unique resources (with few, if any, inbound references or links) that may only appear deep in the long-tail. This is a strategy utilized by many research infrastructures and particularly by those who serve a specific research community. It is quite easy for research resources to become unintentionally hidden and this issue became the subject of one of the investigations carried out in the KPLEX project.

Interviews conducted with archivists, librarians and others working in CHIs revealed concerns and fears regarding the dominance of Google in the discovery of resources the CHIs hold as well as other challenges the cultural heritage sector faces from technology, the internet and big data.

Cultural heritage institutions: The original custodians of big data

Each CHI is like a jigsaw piece in that they are uniquely shaped by their own identity, they are what they keep and they keep what they are,[32] and together they create an enduring cultural knowledge portrait, upon which researchers may draw. As such, CHIs are engines of knowledge creation.[33] Each institution has its own particular remit and mission, which is reflected in its acquisition policy, its user communities and its activities.

Technology has already made a considerable impact on CHIs, as the KPLEX study's survey of practitioners shows (see Figure 1), although it could

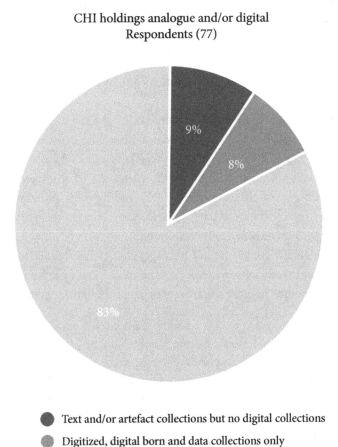

CHI holdings analogue and/or digital
Respondents (77)

9%

8%

83%

● Text and/or artefact collections but no digital collections

● Digitized, digital born and data collections only

● Mix of digital and analogue collections

Figure 1 Types of holdings worked with by survey respondents.

be regarded that the cultural heritage sector is one of the last sectors in the knowledge and creative economy to resist wide-scale transformative digital change. It may be regarded that cultural heritage institutes are the original custodians of big data, just that the data is contained in artefacts and on paper rather than in bits and bytes, resisting the transformation due to the scale of holdings, which archives measure in kilometres of shelving holding boxes and folders and which for museum collections can run into hundreds of thousands if not millions of objects[34] with only a small proportion on display. The challenge of digitizing this wealth of material may never be completed, due to the lack of resources, so it will never truly become big digital data that can be manipulated and explored by algorithmic means. However, the big data era provides a case study of how cultural heritage practices may be changed by influences external to the institution. Understanding these influences is essential to an appreciation of complexity in the knowledge creation process.

CHIs provide expert services as knowledge gatekeepers

Cultural heritage practitioners' role in promoting the use of the holdings they acquire begins with their catalogue descriptions of the items. This process is recognized as being shaped by practitioners' personal backgrounds and their institutional cultures, as well as the power dynamics, of geography, class and gender, which govern the construction of meaning more broadly. However, practitioners' representation of the historical record requires them to be 'neutral' intermediaries between users and information.

A fundamental part of cultural heritage practitioners' practice is helping researchers with research problems and methods. Each of the participants' institutions provided help for researchers as part of their daily operations.

> If people come in with a specific research question, we can point them in the right direction and work on a specific source ... the difficulties we have now are that ... most of our collections are hidden in the sense that the collection description is not yet online ... Once they email, we usually start a dialogue ... because a research question in itself might not be specific enough to determine which collection would be most appropriate. ... We try to give, I guess, custom-made service to guide researchers one-on-one in their research, and once they come here, it's very labour-intensive.
>
> (WP3 INT3)

The depth of interaction between cultural heritage practitioners and researchers, with practitioners being central to the discovery of resources, is essential in helping to shape the research process itself, as they guide researchers through the complexity of the resources and knowledge held.

Clearly, what a CHI can provide to aid a visiting researcher is considerably more than the query–response mode of a Google search remotely. However, in particular, uses of archival data were found to be changing as a result of the increased online visibility of descriptive metadata, research artefacts themselves and/or their underlying data. Researchers were approaching practitioners with more refined questions:

> They are even coming to the reading room with [resource identifiers[35]] to see documents. So, it's a new approach, because ten years ago, people would have to come to the reading room and ask if we have some information on a particular subject, and so on. And now, they come with a list of documents that they want to see.
>
> (WP3 INT2)

Digital methods of communication are playing an important role in improving the discoverability of complex cultural heritage research resources, increasing both the speed of direct communication and the numbers of individuals supported, with a wider geographic dispersal. Communicating with researchers using institutions' own websites and those of research infrastructure portals was a significant channel for the regular dissemination of information (see Figure 2). However, only 39 per cent of respondents to the survey considered that they had a significant amount of their holdings described online with only 9 per cent stating that 100 per cent of collection metadata as available online (see Figure 3).

Practitioners understood that their role will change with any move to providing knowledge online:

> A description [online] can never be neutral, but then researchers can read into them and make up their own minds. If they go into dialogue with us, my colleague and I, we have a certain way of thinking because we know the materials in a certain way. If we eliminate the staff member element in the equation, we will probably get different results. There's a lot to do, we won't be eliminated, but I think our role will also change once we put the descriptions online.
>
> (WP3 INT3)

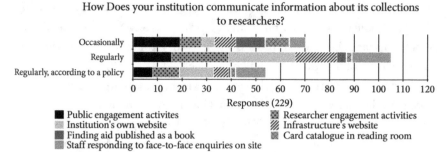

Figure 2 Methods of communicating information about collections to researchers reported by survey respondents.

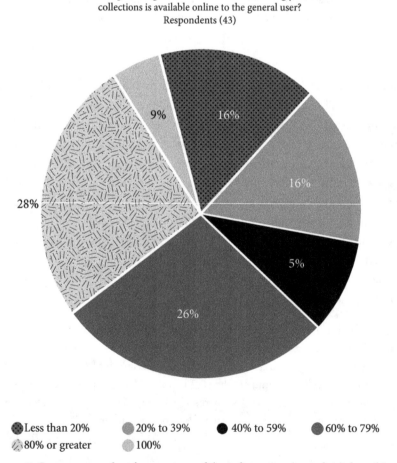

Figure 3 Survey respondents' percentage of the information (metadata) describing their collections is available online to the general user.

Content versus context

A significant amount of a curators' energy goes into creating descriptions, and in the case of archives the collection level description takes priority, containing much of the contextual information likely to pique researchers' interest:[36]

> It's often the collection description that can trigger researchers to take a look. The more information the better, but it's also time-consuming. It takes me about ... if it's a big collection, it can take up to two or three days to make a collection description. ... We try to put the context into the collection description. That's one of the necessities.
>
> (WP3 INT3)

> The context where a document comes from is very important for interpreting it. And also, if you just draw out some document from this and there and so on you don't have a wide view of the whole, you just have this singular document and it can be misleading ... That's also why we try to make out the provenance of our holdings or write something about it. We not only describe it but we also write about where it comes from, how it came to us, and how it came into existence. Was it a collection of a researcher or is it the documents of an organization?
>
> (WP3 INT1)

Description therefore plays a fundamental role in researchers' discovery of material valuable for their research. A consequence of this researcher need for discovery is that many of the early research infrastructures concentrated on aggregating and republishing descriptions of research resources rather than aiding and encouraging the 'publishing' of digitized versions of the *objects themselves*. For researchers investigating archival materials, context can be important in assessing the trustworthiness of the source; how the documents were gathered and by whom, why and when.

Curation goes beyond the basic description of an object and its context with other objects. An expert curator may add knowledge of individual's name changes (due to marriage or migration), variation in spelling and translation not found in a document, or provenance in terms of the journey taken by the object. General search engines cannot second-guess missing knowledge and discovery would not be possible without the expertise. Furthermore, a curator with subject expertise may identify additional resources of which the researcher had no knowledge and may not be identified through the finding aids. A finely crafted representation of context may provide the foundations of sound research but researchers' experience and habits of exploring archival resources could be considered significant:

> The [collection] description is so important and has to be standardized so that you get the same information from every collection description. We've discussed building a hierarchy in the portal website to show researchers where a specific document is physically, but … it's not that important anymore. Once you know the context of a collection and you know in which folder the document is, that's often all the context they need.
>
> (WP3 INT3)

CHIs are trying to make their holdings more accessible through various digital and non-digital means (see Figure 2); however, when only 9 per cent have their entire catalogue available online (see Figure 3), then significant quantities of potentially valuable resources are hidden from search engines and even for visitors to the institutional websites. Therefore, archives should consider changing their core practices to make their cultural heritage holdings more accessible:

> I believe there will be a need to think about … different strategies to make stuff even more easy and accessible but which will have to be … outside the classical description [but rather] narrative-based introduction to collections … making people a bit curious … But even at best, we try our best, they will not be, I mean, completely usable by anybody … there will be a limit to what we can explain by our type of description.
>
> (WP3 INT6)

The challenge for institutions, which use a hierarchy of description for their holdings, is that users are being hyper-transported into the bowels of the archive by a search engine with little descriptive context at the deeper levels of catalogue description, rather than experiencing the more atmospheric and contemplative guided journey down the carefully custom-wrought ladders of the collection descriptions. This practitioner's concept of 'layers of documentation with pop-up explanations' (WP3 INT6) requires additional effort on the part of the institutions; therefore, they must prioritize what they are able to offer to different user groups and how those users work with their material and metadata: 'one size fits all' is cheaper and quicker to build. There is a tension between the traditionalists and those who appreciate that the approach to resource discovery is evolving:

We have archivists here, really traditional, who think that that the context is the only thing that users need. And so, they must have access to the archives with the logic of an archivist and with the logic of the ... hierarchy ... others say, no, people are researching with keywords, and they're searching for specific documents and they don't need to have more information about the context and they don't understand the way that archivists are organising archive documents, so that it's not necessary to keep the context. We think here that a good way to work is between both options, so to develop a tool which gives the opportunity to make a search with keywords, and maybe to make a more specific search.

(WP3 INT4)

Researchers needed to be conscious of their choice of approach and be skilled in carrying it out. In practice, even where a dual approach was adopted, the balance was seen to have swung in favour of the key word search:

For historians, for example, it's really important, but the fact is that the problem is that now even researchers, even historians are making their search with keywords and not with the logic of archives.

(WP3 INT4)

Consequences for users were, however, largely framed in terms of the benefits of discoverability and independence that came with digital dissemination:

But generally, it made a big difference with our database on the internet. People have different requests, more concise. They don't ask, do you have anything about this? They ask, can I have access to this and that? ... They will search on their own and we have less work on this part.

(WP3 INT1)

The user engagement functions of the CHIs are changing, but this may mean that the tacit knowledge of the gatekeeping practitioners is, at best, underutilized and at worst lost as staff retire or are redeployed. Staffing levels in relation to researcher enquiries can be an everyday challenge:

We try to [engage with researchers] but we have a limited staff. So, in the local depot or here [in the national archive], you can ask questions. 'I need that', 'can you help me with that?', and so we talk with the persons and we try to help. [We suggest a] source can be helpful ... When you have a problem with our digital archives, you'll have to fill in a form and maybe one half-hour per day I respond to these questions, but the responses are very standardized because we can't go in. We don't have the staff to go into all the difficulties of their questions, so you give general directions.

(WP3 INT7)

Researchers' experience of this archive was less personalized as a result of the high ratio of users to practitioners, and although they might be engaged in a dialogue with an archivist, it was likely to be of a more instrumental nature, with a requirement on the researcher to stimulate and steer the process. Therefore, in this case of an overstretched archive, it would be more efficient and more fruitful if the researcher first engaged via online searches of the institution's catalogue.

CHIs have been cataloguing their holdings and giving context, for their entire existence, and this has evolved into institutional specific methodologies often based upon national requirements and standards which have transfigured into digital versions maintaining the vagaries of past practice.

Metadata was seen by practitioners as one of the vehicles for conveying context to the user but using systems that were fit-for-purpose and enabling the user to travel between perspectives also played a role:

I think generally it's useful if in the way you sort of structure your information you can capture relationships between objects and even things that aren't objects … Neither our systems nor our metadata is sort of properly set up to [provide this context]. So, in that sense I see less value in just describing an item on its own and more value in trying to in the way collections are put together, made available, to sort of build some of those links or make them more visible.

(WP3 INT10)

External influences were cited as the catalyst for adopting greater standardization of metadata, as this account illustrates:

Before we introduced the international standard archival descriptions, we used a customized metadata schema. When the museum was created in 1994, the archival description was not meant as an archival description. The staff members were collecting objects – photos, documents – to make the permanent exhibition. They created a metadata schema especially focusing on what is the topic of this photo or this document, where could we put it in the museum, what is the keyword so we can quickly find it to put it in the layout of certain panels. When we made a transition in 2012, we did a mapping to see which fields were in the old schema and we tried to combine fields to fit the international standard, and that actually worked.

(WP3 INT3)

Standardization is challenging for all institutions as it not only costs time, effort and money, all of which are in short supply in CHIs,[37] but also exposes previous mistakes in methodologies utilized and variation in practitioner practice.

Spacelessness, placelessness and hypertravel

Most CHIs have a situated production (creation or holding) and consumption (observation) relationship with the population[38] that funds their activities and visits their physical location(s), be it at a national or local level. Their collection policy may often reflect this relationship, and the manner in which the institution was established. A national archive will hold documents of state and others of national significance, whereas a local museum may hold objects which may once have belonged to local dignitaries and luminaries, local archaeological finds, or related to local industries. Topic-specific CHIs will also usually have a national or local historic place-centred remit. Clearly there are examples where the institution's holdings are not, by and large, related to the place, in which they are located – famous examples being the Pergamon Museum[39] and the British Museum,[40] where collections were built upon the amassing of items by their respective nationals. Archive-museums such as Yad Vashem,[41] located in Israel, have a global subject-specific collection policy which includes the copying of archival documents on the Holocaust from other institutions.

This traditionally location-centric nature of CHIs' activities supporting researchers has been greatly altered by the Web, the internet and faster new forms of telecommunications available. The notion of distance is rendered meaningless by telemediation, or rather it does 'significantly disrupt the spatial logic of modernist societies'.[42] Moreover, Dodge and Kitchin argue that 'time is becoming *the* crucial dimension of who is accessible, rather than geographic location'.[43]

With financial resources and available time becoming a limiting factor for researchers, travelling to CHIs can be targeted and made meaningful by utilizing the institution's online catalogue. The initial discovery phase of the research lifecycle may be made more efficient with specific judicious questions asked by the researcher after accessing the online catalogue, rather than a 'general question like, do you have something about Holocaust?' (WP3 INT8) first and seeking guidance from the archivists as to the possibilities for narrowing their exploration.

While the research process still involves a dialogue between practitioners and researchers, online catalogues have shifted the balance of control towards the user. For smaller institutions that had not previously enjoyed exposure to a wide audience, datafication of finding aids and online catalogues has expanded the proportion of material used:

> Because before people ask only for the same documents and the same collections. Thanks to the digital library and the publication of the inventories we recorded an interest for other collections that before [had] no requests, not requested or very rarely requested. So, the digital library is a very good … vehicle to make known all that we hold.

(WP3 INT8)

It may be argued that with the placelessness of the online resources, both catalogues and digitized collections, researchers, and in particular early career researchers, are missing the valuable experience of interacting with the knowledge of the cultural heritage practitioners, located with the research resources, and the practitioner's support in developing the research question. Communication tools, such as video conferencing, may be considered to increase the physical separation between the researcher and the practitioner and hence the placelessness of the interaction; however, they maintain the connectedness in a placeless environment. Nevertheless, differences in time zones may still affect accessibility to real-time services and resources.

Dodge and Kitchin question whether that placelessness represents the diminishing of an authentic identity of place and ask 'does cyberspace help render geographic space placeless?' They have 'little doubt that new places, and new spatialities are being formed online'.[44] However, the generated one-dimensional map of results from a Google search is entirely placeless; it does not represent a geographical place or for that matter a persistent virtual place. It could be contended that it does not represent the Google space or place. The context of the links, to collection holding institutions and others, is entirely removed from what is presented, the placeness and trustworthiness of the linked Web page are all but removed, with only the page title, additional URI[45] and a few words around the keywords found being visible to the searcher. The provenance and reliability of the potential research resource are not present and as such the researcher must approach the resource with caution, making further enquiries to establish the value of the resource knowledge.

The relatively low cost, spaceless nature of the Web provides the opportunity for cultural heritage institutes to open up their considerably larger holdings than those normally on display to the public. With so much virtual real estate the challenge comes with the user experience design to ensure that the online experience matches or even betters that of physically visiting the establishment.

As stated earlier, there is little risk to the researcher in selecting any link which does not immediately provide the knowledge required; nevertheless, there is a risk for the CHI in that they may be overlooked. Moreover, the researcher may, when clicking the link, have been hyper-transported[46] into the depths of the institution's holdings online catalogue without any context at the deeper levels and therefore may leave as rapidly as they arrived, rather than exploring the collection description further. The CHI must be very savvy, not just in how they describe their holdings to be search engine compatible, but also how they present their place and services online – 'layers of documentation with pop-up explanations' (WP3 INT6) – to ensure the individual user's experience of their virtual place is the same, or if not better, than experiencing their physical place, although 'one size fits all' is cheaper and quicker to build. There is a tension between the traditionalists and those who appreciate that the approach to resource discovery is evolving:

> We have archivists here, really traditional, who think that that the context is the only thing that users need. And so, they must have access to the archives with the logic of an archivist and with the logic of the ... hierarchy ... And so, others say, no, people are researching with keywords, and they're searching for specific documents and they don't need to have more information about the context and they don't understand the way that archivists are organising archive documents, so that it's not necessary to keep the context. We think here that a good way to work is between both options, so to develop a tool which gives the opportunity to make a search with keywords, and maybe to make a more specific search.
>
> (WP3 INT4)

Google may be perceived as a threat to CHIs due to its cataloguing of the institution's entire Web presence, but it is also presenting the institution's collections in a placeless frame of reference, and as this practitioner states, missing context and other useful resources:

> I never use the search engine when I want to do research. Because in the end you have this, and you see things, or maybe I can use that. And when you go the straight way, and even when the search is still methodological, then you miss things, because you don't look for other sources, which can be important.
>
> (WP3 INT7)

Google as a threat

In the interviews conducted, Google was consistently referred to as a 'knowledge sharing platform' that represented a threat to greater openness. For instance, the traditional hierarchical structure of archival collections, through which contextual connections could be traced, was reported to be losing significance as it was undermined by keyword searching through Google and the like:

> People are so adapted to the Google search that they don't even know anymore that there is a different way of searching. Therefore, we also chose to put in keywords and categories that allow researchers to browse through collections based on keywords and categories … That can give you a very interesting perspective as well because it can show you connections between collections … and it can help you find more proof for the point you want to make.
>
> (WP3 INT3)

There was broad acknowledgement that the changing use of collections disrupted some of the fundamental tenets of archival cultural heritage preservation practice both through Google's presence as a rival source of knowledge and in the ubiquity of search engine use infiltrating archival research methods. Practitioners' support for integrating search engines into the research process was at least partly motivated by a concern that the satisficing return of a Google result might attain a hegemonic position that ultimately marginalized the role of the archive in knowledge creation. Many practitioners expressed caution about the 'quick wins' of the keyword search, favouring an understanding of resources and context:

> You have to get to know your material for good research, and we can aid people with that, [advising them] to look into these sources and these sources, but [even] I learn things. So, I think context is that important … and one of the main problems is that the new historians, the new school who use the digital tools, they don't have the feeling anymore with the context, the methodology of searching. They want quick wins. And you can't do decent research I think with quick wins.
>
> (WP3 INT7)

The support given by the cultural heritage practitioners is naturally seen as a key component of the services they offer to researchers. Loss of this expertise will diminish the value of the research resources and make their discovery difficult.

The commercial nature of Google, despite the impartial appearance of a set of search results, troubled this librarian:

> If Google can do better at discovery than we can then I mean by all means use Google. However, these organizations have commercial interest that we don't necessarily share and there're various biases built into neutral-like looking technologies that will probably skew the perception of what knowledge is and introduce all sorts of bias into it. Even though people believe they see everything, they might see even less than before because they're only being shown the things that the algorithm believes they want to see.
>
> (WP3 INT10)

Understanding and being heedful of the inherent biases, which may sometimes be the commercial imperative of the business, is an approach which both researchers and CHIs must maintain when complex knowledge is being sought; important resources may become hidden by the algorithms. Although this participant was keen to 'jump Google' (WP3 INT8) and become the primary source for their holdings, so that 'Googling it' is not the researchers first thought to find relevant resources:

> To be stronger than Google ... I think this is the challenge for that kind of project. To be very attractive for people and push them to jump Google and go directly to your portal.
>
> (WP3 INT8)

Benefits of search engines and digital cultural heritage

Google has been compared to Johannes Guttenberg's mechanical printing press making information easier to access so that more people could benefit (Kane, 2009).[47] It could be argued that Google et al. have considerably changed the research process in terms of resource discovery for both researchers and cultural heritage practitioners involved in developing new systems.

> And so, the aim is to give the opportunity to make the research by keywords, also by the logic of archives if necessary, with the context, but first of all with the keywords because even researchers are doing their search now by keywords. But when you find a document, then you can see the documents in its context, in its archival context, that's the aim and that's the idea that we see for the new tool.
>
> (WP3 INT4)

The well-known interface of Google and its indexing ability may be considered to be preferable for researchers compared to an unknown institutional search engine (or browse-based system); however in both cases, a researcher cannot be certain that all the 'relevant' resources are returned for a specific search query.

Collections, which were purely digital, offered new possibilities through their fluid nature:

> [There] is a notable difference from my archival colleagues, who are all about the original order in terms of preserving the paper copies because you can't just reorganise a box of papers without losing something, whereas in the digital realm, it's a bit easier to provide different views upon things without making irreversible changes; not always but …
>
> (WP3 INT5)

Although many CHIs may have run digitising projects for specific collections, or may scan documents upon request, digitizing everything was widely regarded as impossible.[48] Moreover, digitization does not necessarily convert the object into usable data so the incorporation of complex knowledge into future research using digital methods may be unpredictable.

Research methods drawing on digitization were also not static and interview participants saw a need to respond to evolution within the digital revolution. Advanced search methods are becoming less prominent due to advances in indexing and the use of natural language queries. This is not to say that the implementation of advanced search functionality in specialist research-orientated services will not be utilized if, when learnt, provide accurate speedy results. One archivist felt that 'the difference and the real evolution will come from the quality', in that, once the 'fashion' for launching digital tools had lost its novelty, only the best ideas would attract attention and investment (WP3 INT8). This could be considered an expensive proposition requiring many iterations to evolve to meet disparate needs and unlikely to attract investment to 'Cinderella' research domains and resource-strapped CHIs.

Beyond the keyword

The digital revolution has brought about the exchange of the conventional logic of the cultural heritage practice, and in particular archival practice, for the new logic of the keyword search which is a sea change for archival institutions, as archivists' knowledge of the deep connections of hierarchical context is being circumvented and unrepresented in the generalized search engines which are so often the first port of call. At present digital discovery is still supplemental to the value of enquiry with a cultural heritage practitioner – increasing the speed and reducing the costs of the initial discovery phase of the research lifecycle for many researchers. How long this situation will last is uncertain, but it will be adapted and the knowledge creation process transformed. The tacit knowledge about the institutional holdings of the cultural heritage practitioner is essential to the knowledge creation process whilst research materials may remain 'hidden' from the digital realm, not being described digitally or digitized for access. Researchers who arrive at an institution's reading room with a list of identifiers may at first glance appear efficient; it does still bypass the tacit knowledge of the practitioner and institution. A more holistic approach is therefore advocated once institutions have settled into digital practices and started to think more strategically about how they might serve the specific needs and aims of the research community more precisely.

If data are the new oil (a misleading metaphor discussed in Chapter 2), then like oil its profits are not evenly distributed with only some benefitting from its intrinsic value. The vast majority of data preserved in CHIs is not held in bits and bytes.[49] Thus, the likelihood that all of the produce of millennia of human endeavour being digitally accessible can be considered to be negligible; it will remain analogue in form for the foreseeable future. The use of computational big data techniques may only be applied in limited and specific ways to data which has most likely been created and prepared specifically for the research methodology employed, consequently never truly big data on the scale seen in other research domains. Reuse may be limited due to the effort input during data preparation leading to an unwillingness to share the dataset with other researchers.

It is important to note the technical differences between Google's search engine and the ones provided by CHIs. Google uses cookies and archives the search history of its users; thus, each 'Google search query produces a wake of collateral data such as the number and pattern of search terms, how a query is phrased, spelling, punctuation, dwell times, click patterns, and location'.[50] These collateral data go far beyond what a user usually associates with her search activities – for example, 'websites visited, psychographics, browsing activities, and information about previous advertisements that the user has been shown, selected, and/or made purchases after viewing'.[51] This data surplus enables a prediction of the future behaviour of the users, which is then marketed to Google's customers and which forms the basis for the placement of advertisement. Search engines provided by CHIs or research infrastructures, on the other hand, are based on controlled vocabulary and knowledge graphs and not on data collected via cookies. In the case of libraries, recommender systems may be in place, but they also do not take previous searches by a researcher into account, but use established indexes or available linked open data to produce results relevant to the researchers. While the differing technical set-up may lead to heightened expectations on the side of the researchers accustomed to Google searches, and therefore to frustrations with the search results presented by an archives' search engine, it becomes clear that no archive will ever provide a search engine as sophisticated as Google's and that archives' technical facilities will never match cultural heritage practitioners' capabilities to answer to the research questions of their users.

Digitized images, or scans, of documents may solve issues of distribution for the CHI but for those researchers wishing to perform, for example, computational linguistic analysis they are less than ideal, requiring further transformation. Whereas a digital representation of a historical photograph may be of sufficient quality for another researcher to reference in their monograph. As one practitioner put it, 'nobody is, like, proud of his huge digitization project' (WP3 INT6) but the essential question for CHIs is what should they do with the digital materials, where any strategy must include a policy where the 'tendency will be towards openness' (WP3 INT6) and sharing digitally will bring together collections and resources, which may be physically very dispersed to create new knowledge and insight. Thus, sharing may facilitate not only more use, but also the recontextualization of materials for example Frankl et al.,[52] and in archival research guides such as Frankl and Schellenbacher[53] and Lehmann et al.[54]

Aggregating the cultural heritage sectors together is as problematic as combining the disciplines of the humanities into one would be.[55] This issue is amplified when considering metadata standards and how they are utilized across myriad research projects, institutions and by practitioners and researchers. Data in the cultural heritage domain necessarily must take many shapes as do the analogue 'originals'. This need is further exposed by the multitudinous metadata standards, as mapped by Riley,[56] at use in the cultural heritage domain. Moreover, continually changing digital processes and developing metadata formats lead to a fragility of digital resources over time, for example, early digitized content which is now getting past its prime.[57] Therefore, CHIs must continually review and have clear oversight of the changing technological landscape.[58] Digital resources, stored in the form of bits and bytes, may become obsolete if new technology implementations and systems no longer support older data and metadata formats. This additional skill and knowledge burden placed upon CHIs could be adjudged to introduce fears that the adoption of new technologies and practices, if it was not governed by long-term strategy, could be in thrall to passing trends. Fragility of resources is of particular concern for digital-born materials and digital research data. As Vines et al.[59] discovered in one study on biological research data, 80 per cent of the scientific data collected by researchers in the early 1990s is no longer accessible. Whether this loss can be extrapolated to other domains at this level, or not, it can be considered a risk that was not taken into consideration at the time, and still exists if there is no strategic coordinated plan on the part of the cultural heritage sector to preserve digital-born materials.

The physicality of a CHI may instil a degree of trust in a researcher, which may diminish when research is conducted through the placelessness of the results of a search engine. For the researcher utilizing search engines for resource discovery, *caveat utilitor* must always be taken into account. The placelessness of such resultant spaces may present the user with knowledge which does not necessarily come with the trust one may expect with holdings of a well-established institution. New opportunities due to the spacelessness of the Web do not come without new risks such as trust in both directions. The digital future of CHIs raises questions about gatekeeping and control over more or less porous boundaries as the historical record becomes untethered from a physical location. Opening access to research data may result in a weak relationship between the institution and its users. Even though practitioners were concerned about the final interpretation of data, digital discoverability meant that their control over the representation of complexity was exercised further upstream of users' interaction with it than if they had engaged with the institution in person. This displacement of the relationship between user and cultural heritage expert in which a dialogue is nurtured (and questions are less likely to be ignored) poses risks to the best interests of both the researcher and the historical record.

This particular aspect of the KPLEX study found a desire for balance in which the historical record was rich with data that could be discovered and used without moral panics. Institutions were responding to new datascapes of research by looking at their capacity to support changing research methods and investments were being made in technologies where it was hoped they would better serve practitioners adapting their practice. The changing nature of researchers' contact with institutions presents new challenges for ensuring cultural heritage knowledge is used to the advantage, and for the advancement, of the world's knowledge.

Notes

1 'Alphabet', *Alphabet,* https://abc.xyz/.

2 'Global 500', *Fortune,* https://fortune.com/global500/2020/.

3 This study further showed that less than 4 per cent of click-throughs happened on the second results page.

4 Petrescu, Philip., 'Google Organic Click-through Rates in 2014', *Moz* (2014), https://moz.com/blog/google-organic-click-through-rates-in-2014.

5 *Satisficing* is a portmanteau of satisfying and sufficing. It is a decision strategy of not necessarily selecting the best-possible option but the first reasonable option, since there is little risk in doing so in a Web environment. Krug, Steve, *Don't Make Me Think! A Common Sense Approach to Web Usability'* (Circle.com Library, Indianapolis, 2000), 24.

6 Quantitative Social Sciences often utilizes well-known datasets, for example, for international comparisons, such as the Household Budget Survey (all EU states) and the Labour Force Survey (all EU states). However, qualitative Social Science may use data from many small sources including archived data.

7 Krug, Don't Make Me Think! A Common Sense Approach to Web Usability, 21–9.

8 Randall, Neil, *The Soul of the Internet* (Boston, 1997), 187–94.

9 Berners-Lee, Tim, and Robert Cailiau, 'WorldWideWeb: Proposal for a HyperText Project', https://www.w3.org/Proposal.html.

10 Nelson, T. H., 'Complex Information Processing: A File Structure for the Complex, the Changing and the Indeterminate', in *Proceedings of the 1965 20th National Conference,* ACM 65 (New York, 1965), 84–100, https://doi.org/10.1145/800197.806036.

11 Ibid.

12 Ibid.

13 A Web of linked data rather than a Web of linked pages. "Semantic Web", *World Wide Web Consortium* (2015), https://www.w3.org/standards/semanticweb/

14 Berners-Lee, Tim, 'Semantic Web Road Map' (1998), https://www.w3.org/DesignIssues/Semantic.html.

15 Berners-Lee, Tim, 'Linked Data - Design Issues' (2006), https://www.w3.org/DesignIssues/LinkedData.html.

16 Kuhn, Tobias, Albert Meroño-Peñuela, Alexander Malic, Jorrit H. Poelen, Allen H. Hurlbert, Emilio Centeno Ortiz et al., 'Nanopublications: A Growing Resource of Provenance-centric Scientific Linked Data', *2018 IEEE 14th International Conference on E-Science* (2018) http://arxiv.org/abs/1809.06532, 83–92.

17 'Wikidata', https://www.wikidata.org/wiki/Wikidata:Main_Page.

18 'GeoNames', https://www.geonames.org/.

19 Maes, Pattie, 'Agents That Reduce Work and Information Overload', *Communications of the ACM,* 37/7 (1994), 30–40.

20 Jamsa, Kris A., and Ken Cope, *World Wide Web Directory* (1995).

21 Jansen, Jim, and Amanda Spink, 'How Are We Searching the World Wide Web? A Comparison of Nine Search Engine Transaction Logs', *Information Processing & Management*, 42 (2006), 248–63.

22 Wray, R., 'Google Celebrates Its 10th Birthday in September – or Does It?', *The Guardian* (2008), http://www.theguardian.com/business/2008/sep/05/google.mediabusiness.

23 Bryan, Kurt and Tanya Leise, 'The $25,000,000,000 Eigenvector: The Linear Algebra behind Google', *Siam Review - SIAM REV*, 48 (2006), 569–81.

24 Chakrabarti, Soumen, Byron Dom and Piotr Indyk, 'Enhanced Hypertext Categorization Using Hyperlinks', *ACM SIGMOD Record*, 27/2 (1998), 307–18.

25 Brin, Sergey and Lawrence Page, 'The Anatomy of a Large-scale Hypertextual Web Search Engine', *Computer Networks and ISDN Systems*, Proceedings of the Seventh International World Wide Web Conference, 30/1 (1998), 107–77.

26 Bryan and Leise, 'The $25,000,000,000 Eigenvector: The Linear Algebra behind Google'.

27 Kosala, Raymond and Hendrik Blockeel, 'Web Mining Research: A Survey', *ACM SIGKDD Explorations Newsletter*, 2 (2001), 1–15.

28 Singhal, A., 'Introducing the Knowledge Graph: Things, Not Strings', *Google* (2012), https://blog.google/products/search/introducing-knowledge-graph-things-not/.

29 'Refine Web Searches – Google Search Help', https://support.google.com/websearch/answer/2466433.

30 Edmond, J., M. Priddy, and N. Horsley, 'KPLEX Report on Historical Data as Sources' (2018), https://easy.dans.knaw.nl/ui/datasets/id/easy-dataset:114127, 14.

31 Browsing and the browse metaphor refer to the process of knowledge discovery whereby the users follow hypertext links (URI), to other web pages either within the same website or externally.

32 Cook, Terry, '"We Are What We Keep; We Keep What We Are": Archival Appraisal Past, Present and Future', *Journal of the Society of Archivists*, 32/2 (2011), 173–89.

33 Robertson, Hamish, 'Engines of Knowledge: The Museum and the Exhibit', *Discover Society* (2017), https://discoversociety.org/2017/01/03/engines-of-knowledge-the-museum-and-the-exhibit/.

34 Victoria and Albert Museum, 'Size of the V&A Collections' (2015), https://archive.li/wip/QyjrP.

35 A unique and constant identifier within the cultural heritage institute to allow a resource to be found. The name for this identifier varies depending upon the institutional culture and the form of the resource. For example, if it is a data file it would have a persistent identifier (PID), an archive folder or box may have a shelf marker, and a book may have a Dewey or Universal Decimal Classification.

36 In the cases of image archives, galleries, libraries and museums it is the object level description that takes precedence.

37   Edmond, Priddy and Horsley, 'KPLEX Report on Historical Data as Sources', 57.

38   Dodge, Martin and Rob Kitchin, *Mapping Cyberspace* (London, 2001), 13–17.

39   'Staatliche Museen Zu Berlin, Pergamonmuseum',https://www.smb.museum/en/museums-institutions/pergamonmuseum/home/.

40   'British Museum', https://www.britishmuseum.org/.

41   'About the Yad Vashem Archives', https://www.yadvashem.org/archive/about.html.

42   Dodge and Kitchin, *Mapping Cyberspace*, 14.

43   Ibid.

44   Ibid.

45   Universal Resource Indicator is sometimes known as an URL, Universal Resource Locator. It is the unique Web address for the resource (a web page): Berners-Lee, T., 'Semantic Web Road Map'.

46   The process and feeling of being instantaneously transported virtually to a new web or internet location without the context of the journey or relationship to the previous virtual space.

47   Kane, Arielle, 'Google the Gutenberg', *The Daily Pennsylvanian* (2009), https://www.thedp.com/article/2009/10/arielle_kane_google_the_gutenberg.

48   Even the digital photographing of objects may not capture the nuances of the object's medium, dimensions, construction methodology, etc.

49   Nauta, Garhard Jan, Wietske van den Heuvel and Stephanie Teunisse, 'Europeana DSI 2 – Access to Digital Resources of European Heritage' (2017), https://pro.europeana.eu/files/Europeana_Professional/Projects/Project_list/ENUMERATE/deliverables/DSI-2_Deliverable%20D4.4_Europeana_Report%20on%20ENUMERATE%20Core%20Survey%204.pdf.

50   Zuboff, Shoshana, *The Age of Surveillance Capitalism* (London: Profile Books, 2019), 67.

51   Ibid., 80.

52   Frankl, Michal, Michael Bryant, Jessica Green, Wolfgang Schellenbacher and Magdalena Sedlická, *Deliverable 12.2: Thematic Approach 1: Edition of Documents* (2018), https://www.ehri-project.eu/sites/default/files/downloads/Deliverables/D12%202%20Thematic%20approach%201%20Edition%20of%20documents.pdf.

53   Frankl, Michal, and Wolfgang Schellenbacher, *Deliverable 2.1: Terezin Research Guide* (2013), https://www.ehri-project.eu/sites/default/files/downloads/Deliverables/Deliverable%202%201%20original.pdf.

54   Lehmann, Jörg, Lorenza Tromboni and Andrei Zamoiski, '*D5.2 Archival Research Guides*' (2015), http://www.cendari.eu/sites/default/files/CENDARI_D5.2%20Archival%20Research%20Guides_Final.pdf.

55   Borgman, Christine L., *Big Data, Little Data, No Data: Scholarship in the Networked World* (Cambridge, MA: MIT Press, 2015), 161.

56   Riley, Jenn, 'Seeing Standards: A Visualization of the Metadata Universe' (2010), http://jennriley.com/metadatamap/.

57 Hill, Mark J. and Simon Hengchen, 'Quantifying the Impact of Dirty OCR on Historical Text Analysis: Eighteenth Century Collections Online as a Case Study', *Digital Scholarship in the Humanities* (2019), https://doi.org/10.1093/llc/fqz024.

58 Also known as a technology watch when performed regularly.

59 Vines, Timothy H., Arianne Y. K. Albert, Rose L. Andrew, Florence Débarre, Dan G. Bock, Michelle T. Franklin et al., 'The Availability of Research Data Declines Rapidly with Article Age', *Current Biology*, 24/1 (2014), 94–7.

5

Data incognita: How do data become hidden?

In the last chapter, we saw how general search engines such as Google return considerably more background noise for any specific search query than usable resultant web pages and how the long tail of the search algorithms hides research resources. This is a phenomenon not limited to cultural material, but where the existence of a class of professional trained and tasked with ensuring access to, and preservation of, these materials enables us to see clearly. We therefore now turn to another such manifestation of high (but potentially misplaced) societal trust in big data, that is the way in which analogue disconnected digital collections can sometimes become detached from their function as input into knowledge and identity formation processes. Cultural heritage institutions (CHIs) are moving to meet the new challenges of the digital world but there are yet more ways in which cultural heritage resources can be concealed from the researcher. To make their holdings digitally accessible and machine-readable CHIs must remove the aspects of hiddenness that reduce discoverability and accessibility for their users.

We use the term 'hidden' here not to imply active choices but to speak of the result: that data and cultural heritage resources are not visible to researchers who might otherwise use them. In asking why data are not used we are concerned with all factors that may lead to data becoming 'hidden' from the historical record. Such hiddenness will necessarily take many forms on a spectrum from inconsistent cataloguing practices, or a loss of institutional expertise, to the obvious forms of concealment when data has a privacy dimension, or being more obfuscated or 'buried' in a way that diminishes researchers' chances of discovery. Cultural heritage practitioners are fully aware of many of these issues. These forms of 'hiddenness' exacerbate the discoverability challenges faced by researchers and particularly when search engines are the predominant means of discovery.

In this chapter, we will discuss the challenges caused by hidden data, as well as how data and research infrastructures can aid data discovery and reuse for researchers, beyond the *de facto* Google method, lessons of wider use in addressing challenges of biases and misinformation.

Hidden by digital obscurity

Collections at the majority of CHIs (see Figure 3) are hidden from online discovery and an institution's complete holdings can only be revealed by other means.[1] There is apprehension that the utility of online catalogues and search engines could mask problems of discoverability where context is not clear:

> I would argue that in some ways context is even more important [when researchers find holdings by drilling down directly from metadata] because the problem is I'm not necessarily confident that we have metadata records for everything we have. I'm certainly not confident that you can find everything we have using our systems and only a very small percentage of our collections in total are digital. And an even smaller percentage we can make available online for example and I'm concerned, as is, I think, the head of our curators, that that sort of skews the view of what we have.
>
> (WP3 INT10)

One of the consequences of digital discoverability for users of this national library is a shrunken perception of available knowledge. It could be argued, however, that neither users nor practitioners have ever held a grand vision of the library's total holdings, because they are often built up over centuries in a number of amalgamated institutions. This is especially the case given the compounded obfuscation of incomplete metadata and inadequate systems, and thus these are not resources that have been lost *per se*. Hidden by obscurity is not necessarily an aspect of knowledge specifically being in, or missing from, the digital domain but is a challenge if search engines are the primary discovery mechanism.

In practitioners' experience the work left to do to achieve digital openness means that, for much of the knowledge they hold, creating the possibility of online discovery was the ambition:

> I think the most important part of our job now is ... to create collection descriptions and to put the collection descriptions online so that they are see-able, that they are visible, because we talked about hidden data and hidden collections, and they deserve to be seen. I think for the next [few] years, that will be the focus point ... That's our future.
>
> (WP3 INT3)

Hidden by working practices

Occasionally knowledge is hidden by working practices in the institution, where for convenience the practitioners tend to use the digitized holdings:

> But we mostly use digitised, so some documents are less used, not because they are less important, but just because they are not digitised. That's a problem. But we cannot digitise everything, it will take money and time. But, I think there's consequences on the research and on the use of the documents ... Of course, we try to digitise the most important, or the most requested document, but that's not really possible for everything.
>
> (WP3 INT2)

Archivists as well as researchers are thus becoming more familiar with digital holdings as they eschew what may sometimes be troublesome non-digital material. Thus, a Matthew effect[2] is established where only a limited subset of the institutional holdings is available online and consulted on a regular basis.

> You can say well it doesn't really matter if people don't realise, we have much more, but it limits use of our collections and it also skews research towards what's easily available, properly catalogued, easy to find and ideally available freely online because that's what researchers will go to because it's just the most convenient.
>
> (WP3 INT10)

The first threat to the survival of knowledge in the cataloguing and metadata creation process is that some data is hidden and likely to remain so because it had not been captured initially. For example, a potential problem for those concerned with accurately representing the life cycle of cultural heritage data is the 'almost entirely hidden' nature of aspects of preservation, with metadata creation described as 'something that few people care about' (WP3 INT6). It is thus inevitable that an overwhelming amount of data, that does not become formally recorded as metadata, is stored as embodied knowledge with individual cultural heritage practitioners. The data is then hidden because – although it is possible to make it machine-accessible and searchable – this is not considered when it comes to describing and therefore the groundwork is not laid.

Hidden by inconsistent methods of description

Methods and fashions in resource description creation in institutions vary over time. These changes are most obvious with the introduction of digital recording of the catalogue inventory. Moreover, institutions may circumvent the standards introduced by software cataloguing applications to complement their historic practices, as this librarian describes:

> And I think that it's the diversity of the collections and operating at that large scale and having lots of stuff that's been catalogued to different standards in the 18th century or the 19th century, even I mean over the 20th century cataloguing standards have changed. So, there are quite a few challenges. It's both combinations of the systems not suitable or the system in the way how we are currently forced to use it not being suitable.
>
> (WP3 INT10)

There was even variation amongst colleagues in how they worked:

> I do a few hundred of those inventories and [this work is hindered] when the same colleagues come with the same faults, so that's hidden. I think it's a good example. One of the points in the inventory is who did what? And now they are very tolerated, so it was the archivist [B], twenty years ago, made the first list. Archivist [A] adapted it. It was colleague [C] who typed the inventory, read it and so on and so on. (WP3 INT7)

It was this kind of individual labour of activating embodied knowledge that was felt to be the most hidden aspect of archival and object description as its value was largely neglected. Attaining uniformity across individual practices within an institution was an ongoing process for some and regulating this standardization was said to be time-consuming:

> Now we try to use the software to make what we have even more standardised than now. To make that they can't do their own thing anymore. So, then we have to be the bad guys but it has to be done.
>
> (WP3 INT7)

Even when a recognized international metadata standard has been adopted for the majority of holdings, it is not necessarily suitable for other collections.

> I mean the issue that we have is that we have very large scale and lots of different stuff, in particular I mean monographs, books, journals are all pretty nicely

captured in standard library systems. Standard library systems don't do so well on archival material and therefore you then end up having separate systems.

(WP3 INT10)

In such a situation metadata normally collected for an appropriate standard is not collected, or the standard is incorrectly utilized, and thus, this leads to a paucity of information about a research resource. Therefore, it could be concluded that discoverability is reduced and the resource is nominally hidden from a search that would normally reveal it to the researcher.

Hidden by a loss or unavailability of expertise

As discussed in Chapter 4, the exchange of the conventional logic of the archive in CHIs for the new logic of the search engine is a sea change for cultural heritage practice. Archivists' knowledge of the deep connections of hierarchical context must either endure, while no longer being reflected in the search-dominated representation of knowledge and researchers' methods, or it will become entirely redundant. It may be that the archive environment will become a hybrid of deep hierarchical structures represented in the flat linear space of search results. Will researchers be able to make the cognitive leap from the flat to the hierarchical when presented with the search results list or will they simply ignore the spacelessness in their quest for an answer to the query typed? If the context of the holdings becomes hidden when users drill down in this way, archivists' crafted narratives, which attempt to give items 'a shape, a pattern, a closure – to end their inevitable openness, close off their referents',[3] will lie dormant. This may result in a lack of understanding of potential uses for items or may result in incorrect assertions and connections to other resources.

'Google lookalike' (WP3 INT7) searches would marginalize sources that with the aid of specialist intervention would help researchers to discover in the institution's holdings. The separation of researcher from the source of collections knowledge held embedded within the curators may then diminish the quality of research conducted. Even if the balance does not swing all the way from a staff of 'historically correct' practitioners to one of results-orientated clinicians, it was considered that the growing presence of colleagues working from a position of computational thinking[4] presented challenges for conventional archivists.

This manager of research services at a major library recognized the challenges presented by the introduction of technology and the likely ensuing skills shortage:

> And when people expect to get the sort of digital full text type image, we'll probably see rapid changes for which the sector isn't always quite prepared in terms of skills. We're not overly agile in terms of our structures and we'll probably see a lot of shifts where people who believe that their job is secure forever will suddenly find that they'll be out of a job because we might not need as many people doing cataloguing in the future.
>
> (WP3 INT10)

Hidden by a lack of material resources

A lack of material resources was a ubiquitous barrier to knowledge use that manifested in myriad ways but was seen as a way of life, underlying assumptions that the development of practice and systems would inevitably reach a limit. Funding models are not dynamic enough to offer institutions capacity to fully progress their ambitions, from digitization projects that had to be restricted to 'the most important, or the most requested document', as it was 'not really possible for everything' (WP3 INT2), to the arrested development of tools, which made it 'not possible to do anything and so it's not sufficient, it's not enough' (WP3 INT4). Under-funding could also nip innovation in the bud, as this practitioner had found

> the problem is that we are totally understaffed. We don't have enough people to really start an ambitious policy and ambitious management of our metadata, that's the problem ... we participate in research projects about crowdsourcing, but the problem is that we don't have money here in the institutions to develop crowdsourcing tools ... sometimes we have a real lack of information in the caption of the pictures [held in the archive], and crowdsourcing would be a really good solution, but we really don't have money to develop a specific tool. So that's frustrating sometimes because we have the will, we have the ideas here, but we don't have the way to concretize what we would like to do, and that's really the biggest problem.
>
> (WP3 INT4)

Opportunities to reap significant returns were therefore missed for want of what may be a relatively negligible investment. This could hold institutions back from their goals of sharing their collections, as complex work such as conforming to standards could not be easily resourced.

Over-stretching was thought to be a particular problem for smaller archives without a critical mass of staff or the institutional infrastructure to support developments in practice.

> The persons and the money to cooperate with something like [an infrastructure project]. It's possible for us, but for smaller archives it might be problematic because they don't have the persons or even don't have a database where they describe their holdings. They might have, I don't know, a book.
>
> (WP3 INT1)

Smaller institutions were therefore at risk of becoming marginalized as they drifted away from the orbit of the standards and technological developments used by better-resourced institutions.

Practitioners had been frustrated to find that adopting technical solutions could amount to exchanging one inflexible way of working for another if these tools could not be developed over time. In this case, this was part of a general lack of ongoing investment to embrace digital tools:

> We don't have a structural budget to manage digital collections here, to manage digital environments, and so we must ask. We will receive funds for four years, for example, and so we cannot really have a long-term vision and long-term policy without a structural funding of the digitisation.
>
> (WP3 INT4)

Insufficient investment was a significant threat to the institutions' ability to plan for, and respond strategically to, the digital era. In the absence of long-term security, many took up externally funded opportunities, such as research and data infrastructures, to share resources across the sector with enthusiasm.

Hidden by privacy

It was widely accepted that CHIs must work within the framework of laws protecting individuals, which must include taking an active role in identifying risks to individual privacy:

> The only reservation I have is about the privacy issue because that can be a problem if some data in our database, for example, linked with other data

in other databases, make the opportunity to recognise someone who wasn't recognisable at the beginning in our own database. So ... we must be careful about that and think about that.

(WP3 INT4)

Knowledge sharing is often said to be in tension with the protection of data and this was perhaps most evident in relation to legal and ethical constraints on practice. One participant described being 'bound by certain regulations' as 'the most limiting element of all' (WP3 INT3) when asked how far her role as an archivist could promote the use of her institution's collections. Privacy legislation may have an impact on the hiddenness of certain materials as even the archival descriptive metadata may risk revealing personal data:

> We're currently discussing if we can put only the collection description fully available online ... Unfortunately, every collection description has a biography of the person who donated it, and [there is national] privacy legislation that prevents you from publishing certain information. If the donor's still alive, in some cases that can be difficult. We are currently discussing if we can just publish it and see what happens. Maybe nothing happens. Usually, donors are very honoured to be acknowledged as the donor. We don't expect much trouble, but we have to take into account that there might be here or there someone who objects. It hasn't happened so far. We'll see.

(WP3 INT3)

Questions about privacy legislation and the publishing of metadata for discoverability therefore arise as the intentions of regulations and the consequences of compliance could diverge with shifts in how institutions interact with their users.

The dark side of discoverability

> You don't know what kinds of tools are going to be out there that will allow you to draw conclusions that won't have been recognised previously, and it does put people off making data available, even anonymised data, because people are often making this available openly.

(WP3 INT5)

Tools, such as those used in big data knowledge extraction techniques, may make incorrect assertions even if these are not driven by the intent of the researcher or the CHI. If this concern is widely held amongst practitioners, limiting access may become the *de facto* standard practice for any contemporary materials and data. This would be customary privacy practice for data about the living, which is normally guaranteed in law,[5] but may also need to extend to the parents and grandparents of living persons. Examples are bystanders[6] and those accused, but not found guilty, of crimes, and their close descendants who may not know of the accusations. Moreover, how individuals are categorized when involved in such events, and how their actions are evaluated and interpreted, changes over time, adding yet another layer of complexity to cultural heritage resources.

Digital discoverability of certain archival materials may increase the vulnerability of holdings to 'bad use', as one practitioner put it, such as Holocaust denial but the answer was thought to be found in greater sharing: with the exposure of 'vivid' narratives the key to undermining the twisting of historical sources to undesirable political ends (WP3 INT2). The risks of the digital environment and the legal duty for CHIs that hold contemporary history

What are the three greatest challenges that prevent
your institution from sharing more information?
Responses (79)

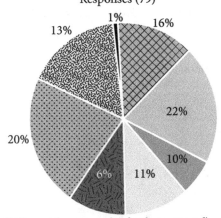

◇ Financial resources (explicitly mentioned)
◦ Additional staffing (explicitly mentioned)
● Skills shortage (capability of staff)
   Modernizations (old methods, processes or back-catalogue updating)
◖ Quality & consistency (generally of descriptions of resources)
⊛ IPR & legal/privacy/ethics
❋ Technical (modernization and capacity)
● Communications

Figure 4 The greatest challenges that prevent survey respondents' institutions from sharing more information.

materials should not be underestimated, especially as they present additional staff-learning and financial pressures for the institutions at a time when they are already under pressure to do more with less. As can be seen in Figure 4, legal, privacy, ethical and intellectual property rights are practitioners' biggest concerns in sharing more information, second only to the need for more staffing. Adhering to existing legal and ethical principles cannot guarantee outcomes in an unknown landscape of data linking and sharing, which unsurprisingly may lead to data being held back and hidden out of fear of its potential uses.

Strengthening the institution's digital infrastructure and staff capabilities is seen as essential in assisting researchers who may not discover what they are looking for in the online catalogue (or finding aid), as well as safely making use of more sensitive materials.

> It should be both, partly in simply improving our structure and I mean the more stuff you make available in digital form, either through download or APIs or other approaches, will allow more computational research in our collections. ... So that has a sort of personal component but we need to develop both the infrastructure and also our ability to support that type of research.
>
> (WP3 INT10)

Reservations expressed about the big data era brought to light another crucial risk limiting openness in sharing access to resources. Data might be required to

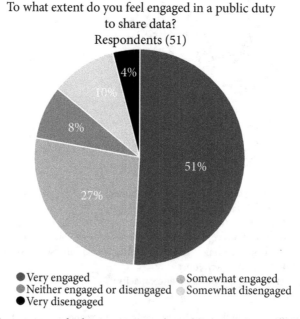

Figure 5 The extent to which survey respondents felt engaged in a public duty to share data.

be hidden as a consequence of certain types of sharing, linking of resources and the potential for automated assertions which may be erroneous or disclosive.

Most practitioners identify a public duty to share data, with which they feel engaged (see Figure 5). Aggregation of information from different CHIs was thought to be relevant to institutions' particular operation and goals and there is a high level of involvement with, and interest in, research infrastructure and aggregation projects.

Discovery through cultural heritage institutional involvement in (European) data and research infrastructures

Data and research infrastructures[7] are also addressing the challenges of resource discovery for their designated research communities. Discoverability and interoperability between datasets were the primary stimulators for the establishment of many research infrastructures in the humanities and social sciences. However, they have many more functions in supporting communities of research data users and knowledge-holding institutions. Many of the research infrastructures aggregate heterogeneous data with the aim of consistent standardization and making it available, not only via their own indexing algorithms, but also potentially making it available to other aggregators. It is the unique understanding of the designated communities served that brings additional value to the research infrastructure and resource discovery through, for example, the addition of (multilingual) controlled vocabularies for advanced search techniques. Furthermore, they provide services and development support to metadata/data sharing CHIs in the form of tools for metadata improvements to meet community standards. For many of the smaller or less well known of the CHIs the inclusion of information about them in the infrastructure portals facilitates improved international exposure and enquiries by researchers, an advantage this archivist felt was inherent in being part of a larger research infrastructure that respects the nature of cultural heritage knowledge:

> Because, we have to expose the documents to encourage local studies. If people can't see us, we can't exist, so it's very important. And, the [X] portal also corresponds to the view of the [institution]. It's a scientific portal, it's very human behind the portal ... So, it's the view of the [institution] ... because, we cannot be only for the local researcher ... And, since we are on the portal, we have a lot of foreign researchers, in fact. So, it's very important for us.
>
> (WP3 INT2)

As an external force, research infrastructures acting upon institutional practice were said to be a positive agent for change in institutions:

> In 2010, we had a system where there was one [Microsoft] Access database with item descriptions. Every collection that came in was split into items, and then you had an item description. That was it, nothing else was done with it. Then [infrastructure project] came in and we started making collection descriptions. All collection description items received a unique and fixed identifier. We didn't have that before. We went through this process with [infrastructure project], and in 2014, we had a new work method. We learnt from working with [infrastructure project] what the gain is from working with external partners.
>
> (WP3 INT3)

Shaking up institutional practice from the outside could therefore achieve significant change in a relatively short time. Moreover, the benefits of sharing via a research infrastructure were also seen as reflecting the changing nature of cultural heritage into an increasingly networked domain:

> So our holdings are known better because we have some information that completes the holdings of the other institutions.
>
> (WP3 INT1)

Practitioners' enthusiasm about archival holdings fuelled their commitment to sharing their 'hidden treasures', which they saw as precious but also 'common knowledge', in the sense that such knowledge should be a commons (WP3 INT2). Thus, their involvement in and commitment to research infrastructures could be seen to be beyond the mere financial. This fundamental ideology of sharing knowledge was at the heart of practitioners' desire to participate in infrastructure projects, for example, as:

> You can't stay in your own cocoon to do your own things ... you have to give your data to as much people as possible ... You can reach new people. There is a possibility for new research. Also, for the institution it has a second benefit. You have to be visible. You can increase your visibility.
>
> (WP3 INT7)

There was give and take in this perception, with a generous spirit and European camaraderie driving openness and an expectation of a return on this investment in expanding an institution's audience in a way that it could not achieve alone. This was buoyed by observed successes of infrastructure projects:

No Archive can work like Google. We don't have the manpower or the finances of Google. But to present data in a platform like [X research infrastructure] has on one hand a chance that people are asking for your holdings. On the other side it's a big, big danger that they are only looking for that information and don't realise that we might have more.

(WP3 INT1)

Encouraging the use of a CHI's holdings could be a benefit of research infrastructures, but an institution holding back from sharing fully, whether by failing to digitally publish its finding aid or not sharing all of its metadata via the research infrastructure, may experience a Matthew effect in terms of what holdings get used.

Research and data infrastructure projects are seen as a good way to both 'see the importance of standards and norms' and 'have a larger view about our field and other scientific fields' (WP3 INT2). Despite the observed benefits of involvement in research infrastructures, however, there are challenges to overcome for CHIs looking to become involved, as this practitioner observed when considering the cultural and linguistic differences between the communities of practice involved:

The first time that I understood what [project partners] were saying, because I could understand the words and the meaning of the words, it was really a victory. And I really thought, okay, wow, there's a completely different world out there, and if we do what these people say, we could actually share and get collections from other institutes digitally and put their descriptions into our system directly without me having to put in all the metadata myself. That was like an epiphany.

(WP3 INT3)

Collaborating with research infrastructures and other metadata aggregators offers the benefit of an 'outside opinion' (WP3 INT6) and was seen by practitioners as useful in terms of positioning their institutions within the sector. Additionally, being 'forced to evolve' provided 'technical advantages' (WP3 INT7), such as the adoption of metadata standards, which allowed them to conform to widespread practices and not be left 'behind' (WP3 INT4). Adapting to sharing on this level could transform practice and practitioners expressed openness to changing their practice when they were confident of the benefits of sharing. There is no doubt, however, that this is challenging for some who are less capable of adjusting their practice.

The future should not be hidden

Hiddenness is part of the story of the acquisition, preservation, cataloguing, description and dissemination of cultural heritage artefacts and is still a multifaceted problem even with the support of research infrastructures. The additional data generated throughout the process is subject to choices made at the time by the practitioners and the degree to which hiddenness can occur is subject to many influences. The recognition and inscription of values and meanings in cultural heritage are in never-ending dialogue and practitioners make important contributions to this process, working to ensure that the materials in their care can continue to be used to create new knowledge. The use and non-use of cultural heritage resources necessarily re-inscribe the meanings given to them and the value they appear to have for future use. Certain materials will be more prominent or more hidden at any given instance in their consultation, depending upon the route of access. Every such instance, whether the motivation is the faithful construction of metadata, a seemingly passive fact-finding exercise, or analytical interpretation for research purposes, is an activation and a re-contextualization.[8]

Measures required for eliminating hiddenness, and thus improving discoverability, cannot be equal for all data, materials, practice, institutions and therefore researchers. Sometimes the technologies adopted are not fit for purpose, as evidenced by practitioners unable to find data using their institution's own search engines. Generic search engines such as Google cannot know or infer what is hidden or why this might be so. Even with the superabundance of resultant links it could be still assumed that there is a Matthew effect present each time a researcher creates a query, especially with the search engine's willingness to provide the question via autocomplete. An objective of research infrastructures covering cultural heritage is to improve discoverability and reuse of data and research materials, sometimes with a role to support both researchers and CHIs.

As identified by practitioners, presenting data in a research infrastructure gives an institution increased exposure, as more people ask for specific items, not realizing that there are other items available. This is perhaps caused by the institution not fully digitally publishing all records of their holdings but infrastructures must understand that cultural heritage data and metadata are messy, being the result of human activity, rather than that of machine or sensor output. Metadata aggregating infrastructures cannot just insist on perfect records that meet their exacting standards: they must aid CHIs with mapping, transforming and correcting their metadata, ideally in an automated or semi-automated fashion.

Without greater engagement with external infrastructures and other actors, not only will data become hidden but so will the institution: practitioners identified a lack of material resources that prevents the organization from standing out in the crowded field of spaceless search results where all appear equal. This does not mean institutions must indulge in the wholesale digitization of all objects in their catalogue or perish but they must ensure their catalogue is based on the current international standards for the collection type and is machine-actionable.[9] Complex knowledge is at risk of being marginalized, not least because of valid and pressing concerns of inadequate resources across CHIs. Reliance upon funding from research projects with their own agenda may influence the choices of materials being made digitally available, while holding other material back risks the possibility of skewing the public perception and researcher expectations of the institution's holdings. Recognizing all of the institution's existing hiddenness challenges resulting from both active and passive practices, and having a strategy towards discoverability for holdings, is essential to maintaining relevance in the digital environment.

The options for digital discoverability of cultural heritage resources appear to be constantly in flux with new institutional, national, transnational, domain-specific and pan-domain data and research infrastructures. The wealth of choices for researchers may appear bewildering; which to choose and why is unclear. Should the researcher go to a general cultural heritage aggregator such as Europeana,[10] a discipline portal,[11] an institution's website search engine, or Google for any given question? As mentioned in the last chapter, there is little risk to any individual choice, beyond a loss of time, but access to too much information in too many directions may scramble the researcher's knowledge-gathering strategies. As the research discovery services available mature and start to integrate additional benefits, which act as nucleators for the coalescence of communities, the choice of discovery services will become clear to a research domain. The development of research and metadata aggregating infrastructures may ensure a representation of archival knowledge endures and has a dynamic relationship with researchers' methods. However, for the moment it is not surprising that online resource discovery is mediated predominantly by Google despite its failings for cultural research.

Living, breathing cultural practices require the space to re-interpret artefacts of the past through the lens of contemporary practice. Furthermore, the reuse, remixing and sharing of experimental data require a space that facilitates scholarly discourse and possible collaboration. These spaces cannot be the 'fake news' and conspiracy theory-filled environments of public social media platforms, nor the open public web, as the risk of discovery, misunderstanding, misinterpretation and misuse without context may be too great. This becomes critical when data have an impact upon individuals, groups or communities. Where emerging cultural practices of remix and recombination become very entangled with technologies that follow the software culture ethos and reject context, the potential for out-of-context misuse may have consequences well beyond the scholarly domain, as we will discover in Chapter 6.

Notes

1   Either by enquiring with the institution, or via a publish and printed holdings catalogue/finding aid, or a printed research guide.

2   Merton, Robert K., 'The Matthew Effect in Science', *Science*, 159/3810 (1968), 56–63.

3   Duff, Wendy M. and Verne Harris, 'Stories and Names: Archival Description as Narrating Records and Constructing Meanings', *Archival Science*, 2/3 (2002), 276.

4   Williamson, Ben, 'Political Computational Thinking: Policy Networks, Digital Governance and "Learning to Code"', *Critical Policy Studies*, 10/1 (2016), 39–58.

5   For example, in Europe the General Data Privacy Regulation has been enacted in EU states: Intersoft Consulting, 'General Data Protection Regulation (GDPR) – Official Legal Text', *General Data Protection Regulation (GDPR)* (2018), https://gdpr-info.eu/.

6   Ehrenreich, Robert M. and Tim Cole, 'The Perpetrator-Bystander-Victim Constellation: Rethinking Genocidal Relationships', *Human Organization*, 64/3 (2005), 213–24.

7   These can be local, national or international collaborations of organizations which together provide access to valuable research resources for designated research communities.

8   Ketelaar, Eric, 'Tacit Narratives: The Meanings of Archives', *Archival Science*, 1 (2001).

9   It should be possible for an algorithm to process the metadata without failure, facilitating advanced discovery and analysis.

10 'Europeana', https://pro.europeana.eu.

11 For example, 'Advanced Research Infrastructure for Archaeological Dataset Networking in Europe', https://ariadne-infrastructure.eu/; 'Collaborative European Archive Infrastructure', http://www.cendari.eu/; 'European Holocaust Research Infrastructure', https://www.ehri-project.eu.

6

From obscure data to datafied obscurity:
The invisibilities of datafication

We have discussed in the foregoing chapters how the promise of the data 'deluge' is often divorced from its dynamic relationship with the humans who are both (active or passive) producers and users of data and its conduits into wider cultural practices. The dominant messages surrounding big data often neglect the complexities of people in the process – from HeLa's disembodied *immortal cell line* to the 'artificial artificial intelligence' of Amazon's Mechanical Turk – eliding human contributions to position the outputs of datafication (portrayed as a biospheric black box like a pure Internet of Things) centre stage. This chapter looks at where applying the principles of data science to cultural heritage may take our relationship with complex knowledge. A comprehensive view of the impacts of datafication – both on the archival practices that sustain the historical record as a resource, and on the practices adopted by users of that resource – reveals cultural shifts that risk closing us off from complexity. We examine how the inductive imperative of big data applied in the sphere of business and elsewhere crosses over to the cultural realm as an example of how deference to human reasoning is being displaced, to the extent that the use of AI to determine what we learn from the historical record might soon be commonplace, and why exactly that is so troublesome.

As we saw in Chapter 2, data is often represented as clinically controlled and removed from the awkward complexities of human actions and interactions, especially when it is *of* those things and used to understand them. The archivists and related practitioners who work with cultural heritage data – on whom Cook and Schwartz observed a pressure to be a 'white-coated clinician' they saw as inherent in a focus on the 'mechanics' of their data practices[1] – exemplify the role of accommodating complex knowledge in the data ecosystem. This position makes them an untapped resource in the project of understanding how big data is changing our world, for good or for ill.

Recognizing archivists as actors who influence the space in which they operate is at least as vital as acknowledging the positionality of the researchers who use their services. Furthermore, it would be a mistake to judge practitioners' turn towards applying certain tools to their 'inherently chaotic'[2] world as a failed enterprise because of the persistence of knowledge complexity. As Joks, Ostmo and Law,[3] drawing on Latour,[4] describe with vivid imagery of the complexities of *simply* counting fish (simpler, surely, than shooting them in a barrel), even in 'hard' science, 'practices are fluid and hard to predict ... scientific practices are art forms too [yet] the fluidities embedded in scientific practice vanish ... fluidity disappears once inscriptions get reified ... people start talking about science as if it were stable all the way down.'[5] Such stable 'objectivity' has been much critiqued. Donna Haraway, for example, argued against the promise of 'vision from everywhere and nowhere equally and fully, common myths in rhetorics surrounding Science', which she found to be characteristic of a 'god trick' approach to truth as either total or relative.[6] Haraway instead advocated a 'situated' approach that acknowledges the 'partial perspective', wherein:

> science becomes the myth, not of what escapes human agency and responsibility in a realm above the fray, but, rather, of accountability and responsibility for translations and solidarities linking the cacophonous visions and visionary voices that characterize the knowledges of the subjugated.[7]

As the norms of datafication pervade our approaches to every field of knowledge, the translations, solidarities, visions and voices that occur, receive validation or become subjugated in the cultural data environment allow us to comprehend the tacit tensions that reveal the depth and scale of big data's impact on our culture and our ability to envision what 'might have been otherwise.'[8]

What you see is what you get

The hypervisibility that the current era lends certain data (such as that 'freely available' on social media platforms[9]) has been subject to critique from many quarters. As we have described in Chapter 3, the hyperabundance of data that is being made accessible is not easily navigated but necessitates the processes and tools of sensemaking. In addition, the big data era presents a new landscape where entrenched values, biases and assumptions are hard-wired and coalesce to cast shadows over some of the resources of our collective memory. In Chapter 2, we discussed how crucial metaphors are in reproducing or disrupting our culture. When considering the importance of analogies to AI, Pearl asserts that, despite the admirable accuracy of Babylonian 'black-box predictions' in advancing astronomy, it was the creative power of the ancient Greeks' metaphors that allowed them to surpass such a 'data-fitter' approach in order to 'model' the calculation of the Earth's circumference.[10] Bowker explains the power of the metaphor thus:

> Our knowledge professionals see selfish genes because that's the way that we look at ourselves as social beings – if the same amount of energy had been applied to the universality of parasitism/symbiosis as has been applied to rampant individualistic analysis, we would see the natural and social worlds very differently. However, scientists tend to get inspired by and garner funding for concepts that sit "naturally" with our views of ourselves.[11]

When we apply principles of human thought to new technologies then, as in the definition of AI as 'computing technologies that resemble processes associated with human intelligence',[12] we imbue those technologies with such values. The advent of an era of 'scientific discovery by computer' that 'is totally isolated from all social and cultural factors whatever' was heralded by Slezak in 1989, who posited that AI constituted 'a "pure" or socially uncontaminated instance of inductive inference'.[13] The march of the inductive imperative across academic disciplines has been observed by commentators such as Kitchin, who describes the creep of a 'new empiricism' driven by 'agnostic data analytics' that allow data to 'speak for themselves free of human bias or framing' – the results exposing a pure truth.[14] Kitchin sees this paradigm shift extending all the way across the social sciences and the humanities,[15] areas we would expect to be impervious to the 'myth of big data': the sirens' call promising to free us from human bias.[16] As we discussed in Chapter 3, bias is central to historical enquiry, the historian's navigation of subjectivities demonstrating the verifiability of her methods through the 'persistent plodding'[17] of her own decision making. We have identified concerns associated with the separation of understanding from knowledge when the black-boxed decision making of neural nets' predictive approaches are used – an extra layer of opacity from stochastic data models.

Concerns have been raised about big data tools since long before the application of neural nets reached deep learning's current level of sophistication. In 1993, Neil Postman drew on Frederick W. Taylor's work to describe the principles of Technopoly, which revolved around the primacy of efficiency as the goal of human physical endeavour and thought, and prized measurement and machine calculation over human judgement, which was seen as flawed and unnecessarily complex. Postman was concerned about the growth of the ideal conditions for Technopoly to take hold, namely the appearance of data divorced from their context and intended audience, travelling in no particular direction 'in enormous volume and at high speeds, and disconnected from theory, meaning, or purpose'.[18]

As we saw in Chapter 3, data used by scientists is conventionally collected with the purpose of answering a specific research question, whereas humanists are often inventive in discovering the buried treasure of knowledge in sources that were ostensibly created and preserved for other reasons. The big data era arrived with an acknowledgement of the abundance of data creation that was now humanity's habit and the hard-to-dispute suggestion that perhaps this might be a massive resource if properly (scientifically) managed and used to investigate questions with which it might not otherwise be associated (in the tradition of humanist hermeneutical methods). Researchers were urged to consider reusing the data of existing sources before designing new studies,[19] and the reassuring sanctity of the scientific method in ensuring against incorrect data use, coupled with threats to qualitative research including an increasingly competitive funding environment and 'survey fatigue' among over-researched populations, was persuasive. Archival institutions' moves to accommodate the digital turn demonstrate how strongly societal-level knowledge trends cross into more specialized academic research domains (and how fruitless it is to consider the flows of common knowledge practices in isolation from each other) with the ubiquity of Google-driven search habits the most compelling example, as we saw in Chapter 4.

The standardization of interfaces between knowledge-seekers and myriad knowledge institutions has obfuscated huge differences in the organization, values and practices of those institutions. Many elements of archival practitioners' work go, unsurprisingly, unsung, but the drive to furnish users with detailed information about collections without having to ask for it suggests that dialogic exchange with these gatekeepers was an unnecessary barrier that has been removed. There is a fundamental shift here in access to knowledge and knowledge creation power structures: users begin to feel closer to the knowledge they seek while practitioners drift away from their pivotal position as their grasp of how material is being used loosens. If this sounds like a democratising shift (and we will discuss this later), any such benefit is hobbled by the reality that an overwhelming amount of data that does not become formally recorded as metadata continues to be stored as tacit knowledge in cultural heritage practitioners themselves. The continuing daily practices of responding to user enquiries at institutions with the most developed online catalogues are testament to this tacit knowledge. As well as exposing how the different systems behind standardized interfaces vary in completeness and accuracy, this human labour is a product of the specific complexities individual knowledge institutions specialize in and the ways in which these complexities inform their organizational cultures. In this sense, the continuing reliance on tacit knowledge in unearthing hard-to-find material is not simply a matter of jealously guarded professional identity, which leads to losses as knowledge either is left behind when it does not fit the mechanisms of routinization or travels with the person when they leave an institution (it is also noteworthy that, across the cultural heritage sector, many essential tasks that sit between the routinizable and the professional specialist are performed by volunteers).

The changing use of collections is developing in tandem with new skills and vocabularies through which imaginaries of knowledge might be articulated. This was seen to be deconstructing the research process as data archives as well as conventional cultural heritage institutions incorporate data repositories which, alongside Figshare, Zenodo and others, and with the help of research infrastructures, promote the sharing of data from research studies as separate from the researchers' prestige publications. Knowledge creators' use of these opportunities to share data is creeping up across academic fields but the competencies required for their discovery remain unevenly spread. In large cultural institutions such as libraries whose holdings number many millions of items, understanding the relationships within and across collections can be challenging for the uninitiated. Within the KPLEX interviews, one head of a service team at a national library described how digitization presented the mammoth challenge of impressing the importance of context upon a user who has *landed* on a page without an understanding of how what they are viewing relates to the institution's collections as a whole (never mind the collections of other institutions). It was felt that the library's traditional visitors forged an awareness of the number of *boxes of stuff* that related to their query versus the number they had actually got to grips with, whereas today's user, presented with a satisficing Google lookalike result, has her curiosity curtailed.

Furthermore, independent research experimenting with language technology like Open AI's GPT-3[20] has suggested that a tendency in the popular imagination to value the immediacy of 'solutions' over accuracy in terms of how germane they are to the spirit of a query, coupled with black-boxed mechanisms, creates the conditions for powerful AI to steer towards goals that are neither optimal nor apocalyptic, but skewed by placing too much value on 'quick wins'. This was described on vox.com as 'handing over our future' by mistake, 'one it'd be easy to make step by step, with each step half an accident'.[21]

When working with data engineers to change systems and practice at diverse knowledge institutions, cultural heritage practitioners are keenly aware of the challenges outlined above. Digitization is a much more involved process than the mere production of a digital copy of artefacts and a careful balance must be struck to ensure that, in preparing material to be read by a machine, knowledge complexity is not omitted or dodged in favour of producing a manageable simulacrum that does not do justice to the item's links to – or divergence from – other knowledge, or significant milestones on its journey to the user. Once (some of) an institution's collections are digitized, it can join a data-sharing infrastructure that will take the heavy lifting out of broadcasting its new digital discoverability to the world. These initiatives peel back another layer of context by applying further standardization. Kitchin describes databases and digital infrastructures as 'unmooring' analysis from an understanding of data production and representation, with standardization of metadata for processing by algorithms working to 'decontextualize and depoliticize the data contained within'.[22] For practitioners, opening access can result in a weakened relationship between the institution and its users, raising questions about gatekeeping and control over more or less porous boundaries as the historical record becomes untethered from a physical location. Opening access to the world's knowledge is, however, the raison d'être of cultural heritage institutions. The following sections explore how the tension between a commitment to expanding knowledge and an awareness of the risks of doing so through current technologies manifests in two forms of invisibility.

The minoritized material: Corner cases and downward spirals of invisibility

The imperative for digital discoverability and growth of data infrastructures has led to the sharing of cultural knowledge sources from institutions of all sizes and specialisms, raising the profile of sources of knowledge that had previously been limited to an intellectual or geographic niche. Cultural institutions themselves may experience a boost in their visibility, especially smaller museums, libraries and archives accustomed to serving a local or site-specific audience, but their new profile may not tell the whole story. Digitization is a costly process in terms of budget, time and labour intensiveness, which includes the curatorial practitioners, who are the experts on the collections of a museum, library, gallery or standalone archive, working with data engineers to build systems that reorganize and reconstitute holdings and metadata to facilitate digital sensemaking techniques – with the burden usually on archival practitioners' *upskilling* to understand computational thinking.[23] Despite high levels of cooperation and apparent agreement on goals, institutions often share only a fraction of their collections.

Practical considerations drive decisions about which of an institution's holdings will be digitized *first*, and which are left on the backburner, perhaps for the next phase of a project, in the event of further funding or – more or less intentionally – never to see the light of digitization. Budget constraints are a very real feature of the cultural sector (although experienced very differently across countries, regions and specialisms) and priorities must be set and justified. In making these decisions, however, it is clear that knowledge practitioners' perceptions of the possibilities, risks and threats of big data technologies, up to and including AI, come into play.

In moving away from *the material*, practitioners fear knowledge complexity may be under-exposed and skimmed over. A Matthew effect[24] might then stimulate repeated use of data that is more readily discoverable in a fashion similar to an article that achieves a high position in PageRank maintaining its popularity through this exposure. Practitioners' acute awareness of the kinds of nuance inevitably lost in the distillation of knowledge into data leads them to doubt that the special qualities certain items have to offer the casual knowledge seeker will be picked up on by the mediating technology. The threat here is that some forms of knowledge will not be properly translated by computational methods and, although rendered technically discoverable, the features that make them an attractive, perhaps unique, source will not end up as metadata that provide a clear path for users who do not already know what they are looking for. Practitioners' expertise moves them to further caution through their imaginaries of a machine that proffers some artefacts *too* readily, that is, one that enables undesirable data linking. The dark side of discoverability is characterized by practitioners as the potential for 'artificial intelligence … to draw new conclusions', particularly from unstructured data, which had, until recently, 'resisted the broader analysis'. With this comes the 'significant danger'[25] that the inferences of machine processing and data linking practices that are the data science modus operandi of Google and Facebook could expose identifying data about individuals. Digital discoverability therefore exposes a dark side that archivists are used to mediating as gatekeepers of material that is vulnerable to misuse and magnifies this threat beyond the potential that can be seen unaided by digital tools. Unsurprisingly, practitioners have acted on this understanding to resist certain moves towards knowledge sharing. Self-styled 'data skeptic', Cathy O'Neil, explains this mentality in her message to 'the overly sunny data lover' – a reminder that not everything we seek to understand is

> measurable, that not all proxies are reasonable, and that some models have unintended and negative consequences. While it's often true that doing something is better than doing nothing, it's also dangerously easy to assume you've got the perfect answer when at best you have a noisy approximation.[26]

Unintended consequences in general, and *un*reasonable proxies and *im*perfect, satisficing answers in particular, are at the heart of cultural knowledge practitioners' reservations about datafication beyond the dark side of discoverability. Underlying these concerns is a perception familiar to readers of Latour and Callon's work *How to Follow Scientists and Engineers*, which observed how differences in practice were translated into technical problems that engineers could then apply technological 'solutions' to – a phenomenon sometimes referred to as 'techno-solutionism'[27] (see also Layne's work on the 'cultural fix'[28]).

Simply adapting technologies that have successfully worked with certain data for use with artefacts from galleries, libraries, archives and museums minimizes the likelihood of adopting the optimal approach for dealing with unique historical holdings. Even where the choice of technology is not necessarily inappropriate, AI's seemingly unassailable march across data frontiers has stumbled due to inadequate training. Biases towards assumed audiences and purposes of services lead to user problems such as those experienced by people with Scottish, Indian and even some US accents when using Apple's personal assistant app. Siri was tested in-house, its English language recognition progressing iteratively from the *default* American accents of Apple employees.[29] It is therefore a reasonable expectation that data at the fringes of developers' familiarity will not be *understood* by a machine working towards these foreign poles from the smooth terrain at the centre of its given map.

As we will discuss further in the next chapter, minoritized languages are at risk of suffering from a Matthew effect due to their deviance from the default, and it is understandable that experts in fields whose lexicons use specific terms in a different way from their use in the common vernacular may be alert to the danger, not just of marginalization but of erroneous linking to other meanings by a learner AI that misconstrues such specificities. Language use is a key vulnerability of design for narrative knowledge but the stories of cultural heritage are told through many formats that have proved challenging for algorithms. In 2015, Google announced it was 'appalled and genuinely sorry' after its Photos service labelled images of black people as featuring 'gorillas'. More than two years later, a Wired investigation found that Google's 'fix' had simply erased gorillas, chimpanzees and monkeys from the Newspeak vocabulary the image recognition algorithm was allowed to draw on.[30] As an example of the appetite an extremely well-resourced leader in the tech field has to properly serve 'corner cases' that problematize the supposed sophistication of its AI modelling, the case of people versus primates hardly inspires those asked to put their trust in such black boxes. This dilemma goes beyond corner cases to even more insidious biases in the associations AI is trained to make, as demonstrated by Google Vision Cloud's labelling of a hard-to-identify object as a 'monocular' when in the hands of a 'white' person (with 60 per cent certainty of this – correct – recognition) but more likely a 'gun' in the hands of a black person (with 61 per cent probability).[31] Similarly, an experiment by the American Civil Liberties Union[32] found that Amazon's Rekognition facial recognition system incorrectly matched twenty-eight members of Congress to mugshots from a police database, disproportionately misidentifying those who were not white.[33] These cases' clear implications of racial discrimination (and persistent work by pioneering researchers like Joy Boalamwini and Timnit Gebru[34]) raised the spectre of datafication as obscuring the representation of minorities but other research has shown how this trouble with big data is fundamentally *cultural*: Beery et al., for example, found recognition algorithms to have no problem identifying a cow when it grazed on an Alpine pasture but apparently clueless when one appeared on a beach (see Figure 6).[35]

Of course, casting the fresh eye of AI over images whose use has been delimited by the descriptive text metadata assigned to it at the time and place of their assumption into the historical record offers the possibilities of new uses as well as risks. A recent example is Google's decision to assume a gender-blind approach to images that is potentially liberating for their subjects.[36] While there may have been good reason for a human describer to omit certain details in a given context, the possibility for recognition of new connections is key to the hopeful ethos of the big data revolution. Custodians of cultural knowledge are used to aiding revivalists while combatting revisionists and although repositioning users closer to the data and further away from gatekeepers might increase vulnerabilities to misuse (for example, holocaust denial), the founding principles of memory institutions – to promote vivid narratives that encourage

Figure 6 The uncommon sight – according to recognition algorithms – of a cow on a beach.

us to learn from the mistakes and achievements of our shared past – should extend through its structures and into the human consciousness of the end user. If a technology frustrates such a fundamental goal, it is not fit for purpose.

Still, some knowledge will be held back from the public historical record. Some archives that deal with sensitive personal material discharge their duty by operating a dual public service whereby they make most collections public and offer private logins for other users to access material they have donated on the understanding that it should form part of the public record, but only once those it identifies are deceased. All the more crucial then, that the *boxes of stuff* be created in knowledge seekers' imaginaries, contributing a cultural confidence interval to their view of their subject and offsetting the clinical doubtlessness of the black box with a healthy dose of acknowledged ignorance.

Generally speaking, the struggle between archival thinking and computational thinking and the conceit of routine suggests a profound power shift in control of the knowledge we use to understand ourselves, question our assumptions and express our values in the most quotidian ways. Exclusion from meaningful engagement with processes shaping the technologies opening up their collections may result in a translation of cultural heritage specialists' complex knowledge of material to a purely technical understanding of its existing functions. In order to prevent professionals in the social sciences and humanities from becoming completely alienated from powers that recontextualize not only their materials but their working practices, it has been argued that they must *socialize* the processes they have a stake in, rather than emulating the values of computational thinking.[37] Where fundamental questions of the power to name, classify and direct knowledge must be addressed, techno-solutionism's side-stepping should be resisted. Knowledge specialists' refusals to adopt black boxes whose input is a translation of their goals should be viewed in the context of other acts in defence of professional and disciplinary boundaries, which suggests high levels of receptiveness to the appropriate application of technology to solve discrete technical problems.

In summary, some sources of knowledge may be rendered effectively invisible by their exclusion from data-sharing initiatives, due to either practical constraints, wariness of the uncontrollable nature of the internet or a protective urge to shield it from the dark side of discoverability discussed earlier. Whatever the reason, the result is similar to preserving the solitary copy of a classic film on a DVD in a world with no remaining DVD players, or of a book in a language no living person can read. Knowledge flows are then diverted from reaching a wider audience, sometimes stymied by a lack of resources, which leads institutions to focus on inward-looking, short-term priorities rather than address long-term goals such as sharing, or the use of metadata that resists sharing due to incompatibility with standards used by other institutions or aggregators with whom institutions might otherwise share, or because those who are experts in a subject area and understand and support ways of sharing are inhibited by an institutional culture that does not reflect this open outlook. Where experts do have the power, they may have a particular reticence about the possibilities of data-linking. This may lead to the sharing of some data while other forms of sharing are delayed; this time lag alone is likely to shrink the profile of those sources, leading to a downward spiral in use.

Casting a shadow: A little sharing is a dangerous thing

In addition to the risk of knowledge invisibility through being left out of technologies for data sharing, another kind of invisibility operates through the use of these technologies. The construction of machine-learning algorithms involves the use of training data, classifications that those designing the algorithm decide are appropriate to aid the algorithm's analysis, clustering of results and test queries that help engineers judge whether the algorithm is arriving at the 'right' answers. Human experts make decisions on which training data to use (usually those freely available in abundance, such as text from Amazon product reviews), how classifications are defined, whether and how to weight certain features, what test queries represent expected use, and what are the 'right' answers – all of which introduce bias and data voids into the process.[38] Algorithms may then be finalized when their results 'satisfice'.

The 'quick wins' of Google's immediacy and familiarity are a constant thorn in the side of practitioners concerned with upholding rigour in research methods, and there is a real fear that the celebration of openness is working as a diversion away from both the complex material excluded from it and any awareness that this phenomenon of hiddenness through eclipsing 'openness' is happening. It is clear that the new normal of the Google paradigm is having a direct effect on how knowledge seekers understand how to ask for knowledge, what timeframe and format of information is appropriate and desirable, and what constitutes a final result. Callon and Latour's description of a black box seems more pertinent than ever.[39] What is more, the coming together of the paradigms of the archival method and the computational method is viewed as imperilling archivists' fundamental values if the result is modelled on the algorithms of Google and Facebook, as described at a national library:

> Even though people believe they see everything, they might see even less than before because they're only being shown the things that the algorithm believes they want to see. So, I'm really concerned with that increasing dominance of these organisations that commercial interests will increasingly drive knowledge creation ... [the reproductive functions of filter bubbles] make Facebook richer but society drifts apart much more and I would like to avoid that ... and not be stuck in something that looks a bit like Facebook large for cultural content.
>
> (WP3 INT10)

It has also been suggested that widespread acceptance of machines doing a 'good enough' job would ultimately have a profound effect on the future of cultural heritage institutions by displacing the roles of human workers entirely from significant parts of cultural knowledge flows. Such displacement would represent a fundamental power shift, with the gatekeeping of cultural knowledge moving from specialists (concerned with content) to generalists (concerned with techniques). In this migration to the middle – training technologies on representative data, anticipation of likely queries and testing that presupposes that the least wrong answer is the most right – it seems obvious that the most marginal knowledge will become further marginalized and minoritized as infrequent use is translated into minimal predictions of use. The unusual will become unused and ultimately unusable.

Big data has been conceptualized as a new medium[40] and, in that sense, we can see the potential for otherness to be marginalized in much the same way as television bombarded viewers with narratives of the nuclear family, reinforcing what was 'normal' while diminishing diversity through its relative obscurity of representation. The potential for big data, and particularly AI, to engender and reinforce disparity of visibility in any given setting is at least equal to conventional media.

An obvious example of (already) minoritized knowledge is knowledge about minorities. As we will discuss further in Chapter 7, minority languages are not well served by AI, which can lead to real-world minoritization as in Iceland, where the national language continues in spoken form but has been written out of instant text communication by indifferent tech firms for whom adapting their products makes no financial sense. Some knowledge sources present aspects of our cultural heritage that are under-represented because the collection and preservation of data relating to them were not prioritized as they were not valued or recognized in the context of a dominant narrative perceived to tell *almost* the whole story. These outliers are prized by researchers as their analysis provides the opportunity to make a unique contribution to knowledge (without which nobody would qualify for a PhD). The discovery of buried treasures, whose exploration through innovative methods and new perspectives enriches the historical record, demonstrates the value of archival practice. Such leaps are also the premise of the application of the techniques of big data.

Unfortunately, algorithms' curiosity is more easily curtailed than that of human treasure hunters. As we saw in Chapter 4, search engine optimization (SEO) has shown how editing the content (data) and encoding (metadata) of a website exploits the easily pleased tendencies of algorithms. SEO incentivizes the creation of artificial links and the repetition of 'keywords' that are not necessarily key to the content in question, as well as spamdexing through wholesale reproduction of popular content. The power of attracting the attention of algorithms with specific triggers has been utilized by data activists. The principle of using *too much information* to flood data-processing systems has been weaponized in the cases of Hasan Elahi, who spared no detail of his mundane activities in offering up hourly updates to the US National Security Agency, as well as the initiative to 'cc Theresa May'[41] (then the UK Home

Secretary responsible for mass surveillance of electronic communications), among others. More regularly, hyper-visibility through SEO, although an industry in itself when taken to extremes, is considered essential to sharing knowledge in digital form.

Since academic journals became available online, authors have been asked to provide keywords that will make their work discoverable to knowledge seekers. Furthermore, the practice of quantifying the citations academic writing receives has been standardized and made searchable online as a tool for tracking implicit value – both of the scholar's overall contribution to their field and of the individual text's application to the work of others. Of course, researchers and more general users view, absorb and are informed by (i.e. *use*) many more materials than they directly quote or cite. If we were to view this fact as a *problem* in light of the potential for uncited material to be unfairly treated by a system designed to devalue data lacking in links in the form of references (compared to work that is controversial and therefore highly cited but does not make a positive contribution to scholarly discourse), we might come up with a *solution* similar to Amazon's Kindle Popular Highlights. Kindle users were offered a feature that demonstrates the duality of Amazon's business model as it uses its platforms to both advertise its substantive products and harvest the data of its users. The company explained that it was aggregating its customers' highlighted passages to help readers focus on material that was meaningful to the greatest number of people.[42]

Amazon's interest in zeroing-in on what exact content appeals to its customers seems self-explanatory: people buy and read the same books for a multitude of reasons that do not always confirm a shared interest amongst them. In pinning down their interest to specific passages (containing keywords that can be cross-referenced across texts and easily recognized by algorithms), Amazon can classify readers in a much more sophisticated fashion, resulting in discrete, micro-targetable profiles. If such a model were to be extended to directly accessed digitized cultural knowledge, where might such a hunger for narrowing down *meaningfulness* take us? Finding out that the passages we highlight in a given text closely mirror the pattern of others' highlights suggests to us that we are interested in that text for all the *normal* reasons, just as comparing one's snaps of a city break to a composite image of the most photographed landmarks confirms that we chose a vantage point that is popularly agreed to confer recognizability. We might then ask what effect the overall *composition* of a knowledge resource has on the visibility of outliers.

Knowledge after Google: The agonism of archives and AI

Despite their role as *gatekeepers* of knowledge, cultural heritage practitioners are broadly supportive of what they see as the cosmopolitan, democratic spirit of cooperation embodied by data-sharing infrastructures. The fears they express are not based on power being put in the hands of knowledge seekers but that it ends up governed by corporate interests. When contemplating the paradigm shift of Technopoly – 'the submission of all forms of cultural life to the sovereignty of technique and technology' – Postman invokes Aldous Huxley's categorization of Before Ford and After Ford eras.[43] Henry Ford is garlanded as the forefather of the production processes and capitalist values that have come to define societies in the industrialized world and his most famous apothegm is that his company's Model T automobile was available in any colour 'as long as it is black'. This restriction of choice, from a previous, wider range, represents an aspect of Ford's production line efficiency (black paint dried more quickly than alternatives) that encapsulates concerns at the heart of both Huxley's and Postman's work.[44]

Since George Ritzer introduced the concept of McDonaldization in 1993, many scholars have engaged with its applications to academic knowledge environments, most notably, libraries. Whereas some[45] have proposed alternative corporate strategies to counter the undesirable effects of following Ritzer's model of *efficiency, calculability, predictability* and *control* (which lead libraries to a 'simplistic' approach that is 'out of touch with the real needs of their users' and fails to engage the 'heads and hearts of their employees'[46]), others have called for a wholesale rejection of *value* as determined by capital in favour of cultural heritage institutions' *values* guiding their working practices.[47] To scholars of the social effects of new technologies, any discussion of Fordism or McDonaldization might evoke the scepticism Uricchio describes in reaction to apocalyptic headlines in which '"new" technologies appear in the regalia of disruption'.[48] Today's datafied cultural heritage sector might be most usefully understood as contending with a *Starbuckization* – a phenomenon that takes account of the fact that even McDonald's has shown flexibility in customizing its offering to a local audience, whereas Starbucks has exercised an even greater degree of control over its outlets (not franchises) and total standardization of its products. In displacing the local essence of a coffee shop with a globalized product, Starbucks has no truck with the comparatively adaptive model that affords the Spanish a beer with their Big Mac. Instead, Starbucks customers the world over are choosing from exactly the same menu. This kind of cultural land-grab is analogous with the algorithmic regime, which, for Uricchio, is 'more than "just another" temporarily unruly new technology'.[49] What is notable about this analogy is that this claim to standardization is applied to seemingly inappropriate environments. Were these analogies not already too many cooks for the *data soup*[50] of cultural objects, descriptions and sources, we might consider the example of cookbooks released in the names of popular restaurants, a technology allowing the user to access the highlights of the institution at home, through the convenience of a self-guided experience that will inevitably fall short of the real thing as the chefs' expertise (as well as the full list of ingredients) is left out of the process. Much like the Starbucks offerings available onboard trains, with the promise of customer satisfaction comparable to the experience of having your coffee brewed to order by a barista, the added value of cultural heritage practitioners is undermined and erased.

The foregoing sections describe how big data disrupts knowledge creation and sharing where gatekeepers have some control over promoting the visibility of their data. Of course, there are many examples of developer priorities conflicting with the value of sharing, as in Google and Apple's exclusion of content from their platforms on the basis of commercial interests, judgements of inappropriate content or seemingly arbitrary decisions.[51] The commercial logic of targeting customers by harvesting their data and offering them products likely to be of interest to them is clear. In providing users with a non-commercial service, there is little incentive to reject this prevailing logic: it is second nature for us to provide data to identify ourselves when using an interface now, whether by consciously adopting the data-double avatar that will represent us in our interactions on the platform or by passing through the checkpoint comprising two text boxes that expect our email address and password in order to passively browse a glorified shopping catalogue. Indeed, libraries have always required identification and their online checkpoints appear as an extension of this. Our browsing of sites like Amazon, however, is not exactly passive; through either logging in or accepting cookies, we are actively telling Amazon what we are interested in by letting it track our movements through the site. Without allowing ourselves to be counted in this way, ubiquitous features that now seem inseparable from the services of several web giants would not be possible. Other features have indubitable value beyond popular applications: while an Amazon-style linking to what *others* clicked on or a sort according to popularity over relevance may not suit the needs of a user searching for specific historical information, a Twitter-style sidebar trumpeting trending topics might provide a useful signifier of relevance – appraising not the content that we have been given but the alignment of our interests to what others are seeking to engage with.

The websites, search engines and platforms provided by cultural heritage institutions do not collect collateral data like Google or Amazon do; they will therefore not be capable of performing predictive analytics, nor is it their task to develop AI 'solutions' to highly complex epistemological processes. The aim of cultural heritage institutions is not to intensify users' engagement with their platform but to provide content appropriate to the research questions that are part of knowledge creation processes. Cultural heritage institutions therefore heavily rely on indexes, subject headings and controlled vocabulary and not on the search history of their users. By contrast, the big tech companies' approach is marked by a 'radical indifference' towards content, which is merely 'judged by its volume, range, and depth of surplus'.[52] Moreover, knowledge seeking, which characterizes the activity of users of archives, libraries, museums and galleries, is not comparable to the consumption of cultural products, realized by Google through the selling of predictions of buying decisions and by Apple and Amazon by selling the product itself. Similarly, cultural heritage institutions are not interested in identifying patterns in knowledge-seeking procedures in the way that Amazon has harvested Kindle data.

Algorithms are generative[53] and they are used by the tech giants to stimulate ongoing use of their services. In this sense, Google has no interest in *solving* your query, that is, allowing you to find a simple answer to a simple question and put the matter to bed, any more than Facebook wants you to use its platform to passively check your closest friends' statuses before logging out, satisfied that they are all doing fine. Without a click-through to some other step, AI does not learn: either to reinforce the supremacy of the most predictable association or to lend weight to a less common chain of content in a given context. The incentive, therefore, is to serve our interests in a way that makes more active participation irresistible. boyd notes how data presented to us in certain forms can make us more willing to override a quest for knowledge in favour of that which stimulates us, like a cheap high.[54] A feature of our addictive behaviour in response to such content is that we stay engaged, adding to chat about the viral meme to show that we got the joke or contributing to the debate on the controversial perspective to put right, out of a sense of justice, what we see as out of balance. Much attention is currently given to the issue of filter bubbles as spaces where conflicting views are not aired or engaged with but such bubbles would not grow, were they not pricked by an incendiary counter-view around which to rally. Furthermore, it has been suggested that being surrounded by reinforcing opinions, whether intentional[55] or by dint of an algorithm learning your 'preferences', generates more radical views, behaviour or at least exposure to more radical content.[56]

If we are to be thorough in our consideration of the characteristic principles of commercial data environments and what it might mean for the historical record if they were to be applied to cultural knowledge, we should also note the rationale of trending as a signifier of importance, the prioritization of literal currency but also the elevation of short-term relevance over continuing significance (on Twitter, for example, algorithms will minoritize the representation of issues that bubble under the surface for a prolonged period). Trends are by nature time-bound and consistency and continuity are devalued. It may indeed be a *myth* that those who work with machines and those who work with people represent separate cultures[57] but the agonistic struggle between computational thinking and archival thinking is undeniable.

Future invisibilities: Popular music, unmapped terrain and alternative facts

In the course of our research, people working in cultural institutions shared their fears for the future with us, resulting in (unprompted or perhaps *organic*) discussion of the 'Googlization' of the cultural knowledge currently safeguarded by conventional archival practices. What are we talking about when we talk about Googlization? The possibilities of data use that Google has realized through its insatiable ambition and its power to pour seemingly endless resources into projects that seize the value of previously unconnected knowledge fields have come to be taken for granted. Attempts to rival Google's initiatives, such as Quaero (as a European alternative to Google Search) and French libraries' attempts to digitize their own collections (as an alternative to Google Books), have been either abandoned completely or involved at least partial capitulation to Google due to relative lack of resources (Google has digitized the books of some of France's public libraries in exchange for their rights). The Google model has nevertheless set a new bar, normalizing an omnipotent reach rather than specialization and a near instantaneous rate of output that has changed cultural expectations to such a degree that the 'fast science' methods of Surgisphere were not questioned until several peer-reviewed publications had already attained publication in some of the world's most revered medical journals.

Googlization now seems inseparable from the customization of a service based on data about the user and to turn away from the advantages of such an approach is now as unthinkable as dismissing the utility of Henry Ford's production line. On a basic level, Googlization is concerned with the search engine itself and how the features we described in Chapter 4 become hegemonic. Google's algorithms also learn from its user base to deliver results that are likely to satisfy us, and results can be further personalized by favouring those that have suited similar users, based on what it knows about us, and those other users, from gathering data across its various platforms. The functionality allowed by such vast data banks normalizes the levels of personalization used to create a Spotify playlist or the businesses made visible to us on Google Maps. The duality of Googlized platforms affects what we will be offered when the machine is learning (songs representing two extremes of overlapping clusters of listeners so that we signal which musical path we would like to go down) and when it has figured out enough to satisfice us (leaving home improvement stores unmapped as it knows we live in rented property).

Aside from the risk of inaccuracies inherent in a blunt instrument pushing us to extremes to complete its learning objective or extracting paradata from us when we are not ready, applying a Googlized personalization simply runs counter to what drives most knowledge-seeking behaviour – the desire to be offered something we do not already know and were not likely to just stumble upon. Taking the example of Amazon's Kindle user data (which gobbles up half-formed ideas in Kindle notes even though we might erase them once we are better read), it is easy to see how common misunderstandings might gather pace in a post-truth era, creating a critical mass that could mean a new breed of fake news in the shape of machine-made conspiracy theories without even the intentionality of an original human source. On a more quotidian level, the creep of customization would favour confirmatory, rather than challenging, knowledge, putting ever more weight on the wording of a query. As AI is about prediction, we can expect to see something akin to a smartphone's autocomplete facility being incorporated into future experiences of navigating the historical record. Might we then treat the suggestions of an autocomplete function in the setting of a cultural heritage institution as metadata or even a result in itself? It would surely be fair to report on such a suggestion in the same way as the hackneyed reference to 'the *Oxford English Dictionary* definition …', as this convention also reflects common usage. Data begets data. It is also worth noting that ubiquitous features of everyday technologies, such as autocomplete, are unlikely to register when applied to another context, but can seriously skew our user experience. While in some settings that might lead to us drinking alone in the wrong Dog and Duck, or discovering we quite like two bands with very similar names, when searching for knowledge in an age of 'alternative facts', the stakes are higher.

Stjernfelt and Lauritzen found that entering 'did the Hol' into Google Search led to websites denying the Holocaust (they posit that serious studies do not tend to contain the same letter sequence, and so it would take deliberate SEO efforts to embed it in websites seeking to redress the balance by appearing on the first page of results alongside the conspiracy theorists).[58] Asking the right questions has always been important but in the era of fake news, starting with a shaky research question – or even the first few letters of one – could send you down a rabbit hole. Writing in 2019, danah boyd asks how far this rabbit hole might go, imagining the spiralling seduction of a slick perversion of 'social justice' taking a YouTube user from textbook definition to rightwing backlash in a matter of clicks.[59] A proponent of QAnon now sits in the US Congress and the spread of this outlandish conspiracy theory has demonstrated that the bar for the viability of claims gaining global traction is so low that any idea that simply putting verified facts out there would be a fait accompli looks incredibly naïve, and any attempt to limit access to knowledge in order to preserve elitist dissemination models starts to look dangerous.

boyd identifies the asking of questions such as 'did the Holocaust really happen' as the work of culturally induced ignorance studied by agnotologists. The production of ignorance is a political project, sometimes in the most literal way, as with colonial officials' destruction of files that contained evidence of the British Empire's atrocities, which they called Operation Legacy,[60] and sometimes more covertly. For example, colonial era records from the British occupation of Kenya, alongside which those that Operation Legacy reduced to ash would have formed a more complete historical record, now sit in the Foreign and Commonwealth Office's archive at Hanslope Park. These 'migrated archives' are not publicly accessible (some are classified 'top secret', others are withheld from Freedom of Information requests with no reasons given), creating a data void as (un)touchable as the smoke that hung over New Delhi in 1957. The myth of the benevolent Empire continues to flourish in the classrooms and popular imagination of twenty-first-century Britain and boyd's agnotological analysis of how newly created data voids can be exploited demonstrates just how seriously we should take both the purposeful production of ignorance and the practices that make it easier to reach falsehoods than knowledge that nourishes us. These are overt attacks on our culture.

Of course, the least we could hope for from a serious resource for seekers of cultural knowledge is that it would not peddle, or feed, conspiracy theories but it is worth considering the ramifications of transposing the taken-for-granted algorithms of one environment on another. Whether or not we consider ourselves to be under the cosh of Technopoly's push for efficiency, it seems unlikely that an algorithm would now be designed that deliberately did not seek to enhance users' experiences by correcting common mistakes. Machine prediction and enhancement now range across every medium of writing, from casual email,[61] through Grammerly's business-speak services, to the short story suffering from writer's block,[62] with Open AI's GPT-3 leading the way to new frontiers of sophistication, and bias. AI has now replaced humans in many media roles and, although academia is often described as an ivory tower, academic knowledge creation does not exist in a vacuum and is always, to some extent, informed by popular discourses – funding proposals are often framed by their relevance to current, headline-grabbing events for example, though they are always the product of years of prior research. Subtle shifts in the curation of news articles on aggregating platforms – whether we click through or scroll past – inform our perception of what matters to society at large.

Efficiency then manifests in the algorithmic equivalent of a library keeping its most used books by the front door – maybe even firing the text you have most likely come for into the revolving door for you to grab it without having to enter the building. Perhaps this would not be so bad, after all, when we had to rely on physical tomes, the inverse system ruled, leaving only the least popular knowledge available as that which most suited our needs had already been scooped up by fellow students with the wherewithal to plan their reading early. Rather than the reassuring certainty that we have been left with books no-one else is interested in, however, we cannot know for sure why the black-boxed algorithm has put these books by the door. We might be fairly confident that they are, in fact, the most used books in the library and, of course, this is a special library designed for us based on everything we have read before, but there is a Matthew effect in the black box that promotes the use of the most used. We might then worry about intellectual rigour if we are going to be diverted to *Existential Philosophy: A Reader*, rather than reading the works of Sartre directly but this is not the only level of accessibility on which the process discriminates. Complex knowledge forms will not have made it as far as the optimization process, meaning that only the data that is most accessible for machine learning will be selected for the shelves by the door – all the books that are deemed too deviant from the norm that has been designed for, simply because they are too heavy, unusually shaped or containing unexpected media, are left in the basement stacks.

Hypernormalised hypermarkets of big data: Refusing to be cowed

Of course, if the result of the various kinds of invisibility discussed above was that we couldn't ever find what we were looking for, we would come to see such services as useless, stop using them and, if there really was no alternative, conclude either that the knowledge we seek cannot exist or that we must live under the oppression of ignorance as it is withheld from us.[63] What seems a more likely outcome, however – and is no stretch of the imagination for anyone with an ebay buyer's account – is that we will be the recipients of a product that *satisfices*. Pasquale describes Google and Apple as 'the Walmarts of the information economy, in that they 'habituate users to value the finding service itself over the sources of the things found'.[64] The invisibilization of provenance might be the most insidious effect of datafication because, when presented with irreconcilable knowledge claims, capacity to judge and choose between them will be diminished.

Following the model of the existing tech giants as a way to share knowledge (and at this point there is no possibility of a parallel knowledge market that signs up more of the global population than Facebook, re-maps our streets and closes its ears to Google searchers' questions based on the trends of Tweeters) cements invisibility not only through algorithmic practice. As long as there is commercialization, there will be an element of the secret sauce, not the transparency and accountability of a public service. Perhaps viewing the gatekeeping of knowledge as something not akin to ownership in line with capitalist principles was always naïve and we were enjoying the anomaly of a period of public ownership of knowledge only briefly. It is undeniably the case that academic journals have, until very recently, sought to keep knowledge from the general public by limiting access to their publications to those willing to pay a subscription themselves or, far more commonly, have the privilege of a university affiliation to draw on. The general public's grasp of the latest research was then dependent on what they were spoon-fed through reviews of academic literature in generalist publications and what served an often sensationalist media. Nevertheless, it has been argued that the 'secret DNA' of algorithms should not be hidden from the public but open to public interrogation and discussion.[65] GDPR[66] has gone some way to providing for this.

We have seen the game-changing power of big tech: in calling time on presumptions of gender identity based on physical characteristics and in 2020, a year that will be remembered for racial reckoning in the United States, two of its 'Big Five' information technology companies (Amazon and Microsoft) stepped back from supplying facial recognition technology to police, and IBM withdrew from the technology, which has become synonymous with racial profiling, altogether. Pressure has been mounting on Facebook to take sustained action against campaigns of disinformation that led to the storming of the US Capitol in January 2021, precipitating its move to suspend Donald Trump's Facebook account. Pasquale's plea for Google to make its *secret DNA*, through which it *includes, excludes and ranks* – a power that dictates 'which public impressions become permanent and which remain fleeting'[67] – accessible to library scientists has so far gone unanswered.

The agonistic nature of the tension between computational thinking and archival thinking must be represented in the knowledge seeker's experience. The historical record is a process, not a product and so this dialogue between knowledge complexity and the technologies that might be applied to it should be ongoing. Presner describes this as not only a deconstruction of assumptions imposed on the cultural record but a move towards making space for 'the ambiguous, the unfinished, the differential, the multiple, and the spectral'.[68] We see this as not just living with the discomfort they engender but recognizing that discomfort as central to the process of the historical record and our most vital struggles to learn from it. For Star, being uncomfortable but 'content with that which is wild to us',[69] meant refusing the translation identified by Callon and Latour.[70] We argue that the obscuring practices of a *solutions* culture must be similarly refused in order to preserve untameable complex knowledge.

Leading the conversation with technical specialists and putting their perspectives on future knowledge seekers' needs in the foreground throughout should address practitioners' feelings of being on the back foot in responding to technologies as they become available to them or having to take up resources that do not fit existing needs because alternative models have not been worked up. The complexities of cultural data show us how shallow our knowledge environment might become if we lose sight of the rest of the 'knowledge iceberg' below the tip that big data approaches shine a spotlight on. The inherent invisibility introduced by data infrastructures' context-stripping standardization processes demonstrates how sharing can come at a cost and what appear as freer flows of knowledge may be the result of a multitude of unseen dams. If our knowledge environment continues to develop according to the trajectories of datafication, without the check of critique that deconstructs the pervading assumptions of big data, what can we expect?

In a classic study,[71] white children who had never seen a black child reading a book were shown a picture of a library and asked what the black child in the picture was doing (there was no black child in the picture). The white children's answers ranged between various menial tasks. Not one, students introduced to the study of racial stereotyping are told, said 'reading a book'. The white children's 'training data' had not equipped them to predict this minoritized material and the 'neutral' technology of a photograph only served to confirm their bias. We look to technology because we are aware of the (all too) human propensity to short-cut complexity: from misplaced keys to optical illusions to racial prejudice, we see what we expect (not necessarily want) to see. However, from misplaced cows to monocular illusions to racist predictions, we have seen that the black boxes of technology also short-cut complexity. We described in Chapter 5 how the context-stripping standardization processes of data infrastructures, which aggregate heterogeneous data, can add further layers of obfuscation, and we argue that the threat of obscurity this poses eclipses concerns about human error.

When considering the capacity of machine learning to contend with the art world, Wyse observes that neural networks' categorization certainty snowballs as images are tweaked to marginalize contextual 'noise'.[72] Have we given enough thought to the consequences of using technology that takes Amazon product reviews as its starting point for knowledge? (The *intelligence* of such machine learning will be discussed in the next chapter). Of course, all forms of progress have to start somewhere, and advances such as those building on adversarial image research[73] help to expose vulnerabilities in the classification of knowledge that are perhaps fundamental to the drawing of such boundaries. Nevertheless, the problem of invisibility is not that the adoption of certain data practices, black-boxed systems, infrastructures and associated cultural norms temporarily covers over complex knowledge; it is that, in applying these layers, some of the noisy texture heretofore added by cultural practices is abraded so that holdings may fit together in a way that *makes sense*, and even if it is a more sophisticated technology that reaches back into the historical record to retrieve them, it is in this more governable, quieter form that they will be waiting.

Notes

1 Schwartz, Joan M. and Terry Cook, 'Archives, Records, and Power: The Making of Modern Memory', *Archival Science*, 2/1 (2002), 175.

2 Ibid., 176.

3 Joks, Solveig, Liv Østmo and John Law, 'The Infrastructures of Difference', *Nomadic Peoples*, 24/2 (2020), 323–43.

4 Latour, Bruno, *Science in Action: How to Follow Scientists and Engineers through Society* (Cambridge, MA: Harvard University Press, 1988).

5 Joks, Østmo and Law, 'The Infrastructures of Difference', 334.

6 Haraway, Donna, 'Situated Knowledges: The Science Question in Feminism and the Privilege of Partial Perspective', *Feminist Studies*, 14/3 (1988), 575–99.

7 Ibid., 590.

8 Star, Susan Leigh, 'Power, Technology and the Phenomenology of Conventions: On Being Allergic to Onions', *The Sociological Review*, 38/1 (1990), 26–56.

9 Van Schie, G., I. Westra and M.T. Schäfer, 'Get Your Hands Dirty in The Datafied Society', in *The Datafied Society: Studying Culture through Data* (Amsterdam: Amsterdam University Press, 2017), 187–8.

10 Pearl, J., 'The Limitations of Opaque Learning Machines', in *Possible Minds: 25 Ways of Looking at AI* (London: Penguin, 2019).

11 Bowker, G., 'Data Flakes: An Afterword to "Raw Data" Is an Oxymoron', in *'Raw Data' Is an Oxymoron* (Cambridge, MA: MIT Press, 2013), 168.

12 Nuffield Council on Bioethics, *Artificial Intelligence (AI) in Healthcare and Research* (London, 2018).

13 Barocas, Solon, Sophie Hood and Malte Ziewitz, *Governing Algorithms: A Provocation Piece* (Rochester, NY, 29 March 2013), https://papers.ssrn.com/abstract=2245322.

14 Kitchin, Rob, *The Data Revolution: Big Data, Open Data, Data Infrastructures and Their Consequences* (London: SAGE).

15 Kitchin, Rob, 'Big Data, New Epistemologies and Paradigm Shifts', *Big Data & Society*, 1/1 (2014), 1–12.

16 boyd, danah and Kate Crawford, 'Critical Questions for Big Data', *Information, Communication & Society*, 15/5 (2012), 662–79.

17 Wang, H., 'Toward Mechanical Mathematics', in *The Modelling of Mind* (South Bend, Indiana: Bloomsbury, 1963), 93.

18 Postman, Neil, *Technopoly: The Surrender of Culture to Technology* (New York: Vintage, 1993), 70.

19 Economic and Social Research Council, 'Research Data Policy', *UK Research and Innovation* (2018), https://esrc.ukri.org/funding/guidance-for-grant-holders/research-data-policy/.

20 See, for example, https://www.gwern.net.

21 Piper, Kelsey, 'GPT-3, Explained: This New Language AI Is Uncanny, Funny – and a Big Deal', *Vox* (2020), https://www.vox.com/future-perfect/21355768/gpt-3-ai-openai-turing-test-language.

22 Kitchin, Rob, *The Data Revolution: Big Data, Open Data, Data Infrastructures and Their Consequences* (London, 2014), 22.

23 Williamson, Ben, 'Political Computational Thinking: Policy Networks, Digital Governance and "Learning to Code"', *Critical Policy Studies*, 10/1 (2016), 39–58.

24 Merton, Robert K., 'The Matthew Effect in Science | Science', *Science*, 159/3810 (1968), 56–63.

25 Edmond, J., M. Priddy and N. Horsley, 'KPLEX Report on Historical Data as Sources' (2018), https://easy.dans.knaw.nl/ui/datasets/id/easy-dataset:114127.

26 O'Neil, C., *On Being a Data Skeptic* (Sebastopol: O'Relly Media, 2014), 2.

27 Latour, Bruno, *Science in Action: How to Follow Scientists and Engineers through Society* (Cambridge, MA, 1988).

28 Layne, Linda L., 'The Cultural Fix: An Anthropological Contribution to Science and Technology Studies', *Science, Technology, & Human Values*, 25/3 (2000), 352–79.

29 Zax, David, 'Siri, Why Can't You Understand Me?', *Fast Company* (2011), https://www.fastcompany.com/1799374/siri-why-cant-you-understand-me.

30 'When It Comes to Gorillas, Google Photos Remains Blind | WIRED', https://www.wired.com/story/when-it-comes-to-gorillas-google-photos-remains-blind/.

31 Lyons, Kim, 'Google AI Tool Will No Longer Use Gendered Labels Like "Woman" or "Man" in Photos of People', *The Verge* (2020), https://www.theverge.com/2020/2/20/21145356/google-ai-images-gender-bias-labels-people.

32 American Civil Liberties Union (2018), https://www.aclu.org/blog/privacy-technology/surveillance-technologies/amazons-face-recognition-falsely-matched-28.

33 Snow, Jacob, 'Amazon's Face Recognition Falsely Matched 28 Members of Congress With Mugshots', *American Civil Liberties Union* (2018), https://www.aclu.org/blog/privacy-technology/surveillance-technologies/amazons-face-recognition-falsely-matched-28.

34 Buolamwini, Joy and Timnit Gebru, 'Gender Shades: Intersectional Accuracy Disparities in Commercial Gender Classification', in *Conference on Fairness, Accountability and Transparency* (presented at the Conference on Fairness, Accountability and Transparency, 2018), 77–91, http://proceedings.mlr.press/v81/buolamwini18a.html.

35 Beery, Sara, Grant Van Horn and Pietro Perona, 'Recognition in Terra Incognita', in *Computer Vision – ECCV 2018*, ed. Vittorio Ferrari, Martial Hebert, Cristian Sminchisescu and Yair Weiss, Lecture Notes in Computer Science (Cham, 2018), 472–89.

36 Lyons, 'Google AI Tool Will No Longer Use Gendered Labels like "Woman" or "Man" in Photos of People'.

37 Ruppert, Evelyn, 'Rethinking Empirical Social Sciences', *Dialogues in Human Geography*, 3/3 (2013), 268–73.

38 boyd, d., *It's Complicated* (New Haven and London, 2014); Caliskan, Aylin, Joanna J. Bryson and Arvind Narayanan, 'Semantics Derived Automatically from Language Corpora Contain Human-like Biases', *Science*, 356/6334 (2017), 183–6.

39 Latour, *Science in Action: How to Follow Scientists and Engineers through Society*.

40 Lushetich, N., *Big Data – A New Medium?* (Abington: Routledge, 2020).

41 As Home Secretary, Theresa May championed legislation popularly dubbed the Snooper's Charter, requiring internet and mobile service providers to keep records of internet usage, voice calls, messages and email for up to a year in case police requested access to the records while investigating a crime. Civil servant Eric Finch launched the campaign 'National cc all your e-mails to Theresa May Day' on 1st May 2012, as a public Facebook page, in protest.

42 Striphas, T., 'How to Have Culture in an Algorithmic Age', *The Late Age of Print*, (2010), https://www.thelateageofprint.org/2010/06/14/how-to-have-culture-in-an-algorithmic-age/.

43 Postman, Neil, *Technopoly: The Surrender of Culture to Technology* (New York, 1993), 49–52.

44 Huxley, Aldous, *Brave New World* (London: Vintage, 1932); Postman, *Technopoly*.

45 Quinn, B., 'The McDonaldization of Academic Libraries?', *College and Research Libraries*, 61/3 (2000), 248–61.

46 Ibid., 254.

47 Fister, B., 'Librarians as Agents of Change, Keynote Address', in *Libraries Out Loud: New Narratives of Enduring Values* (presented at the ACRL Oregon-Washington Joint Fall Conference, Corbett, Oregon, 2012); Nicholson, Karen P., 'The McDonaldization of Academic Libraries and the Values of Transformational Change | Nicholson | College & Research Libraries', https://crl.acrl.org/index.php/crl/article/view/16428.

48 Uricchio, W., 'Data, Culture and the Ambivalence of Algorithms', in *The Datafied Society: Studying Culture through Data* (Amsterdam: Amsterdam University Press, 2017), 125.

49 Ibid.

50 Edmond, Jennifer, Natasa Bulatovic and Alexander O'Connor, 'The Taste of "Data Soup" and the Creation of a Pipeline for Transnational Historical Research', *Journal of the Japanese Association for Digital Humanities*, 1 (2015), 107–22.

51 Pasquale, Frank A., *The Black Box Society: The Secret Algorithms That Control Money and Information* (Cambridge: Harvard University Press, 2015).

52   Shoshana Zuboff, *The Age of Surveillance Capitalism. The Fight for a Human Future at the New Frontier of Power* (New York: PublicAffairs, 2019), 505.

53   Lash, Scott, 'Power after Hegemony: Cultural Studies in Mutation?', *Theory, Culture & Society*, 24/3 (2007), 55–78.

54   boyd, danah, 'Streams of Content, Limited Attention: The Flow of Information through Social Media' (2009), https://er.educause.edu/articles/2010/10/streams-of-content-limited-attention-the-flow-of-information-through-social-media.

55   Sunstein, C. R., *Going to Extremes: How Like Minds Unite and Divide* (Oxford: Oxford University Press, 2009).

56   Tufekci, Zeynep, 'YouTube, the Great Radicalizer', *The New York Times* (10 March 2018), section Opinion, https://www.nytimes.com/2018/03/10/opinion/sunday/youtube-politics-radical.html.

57   Star, 'Power, Technology and the Phenomenology of Conventions: On Being Allergic to Onions'.

58   Stjernfelt, Frederik, and Anne Mette Lauritzen, *Your Post Has Been Removed: Tech Giants and Freedom of Speech* (2020), https://www.springer.com/gp/book/9783030259679.

59   boyd, danah, 'Agnotology and Epistemological Fragmentation', *Medium* (2019), https://points.datasociety.net/agnotology-and-epistemological-fragmentation-56aa3c509c6b.

60   Cobain, Ian, *The History Thieves: Secrets, Lies and the Shaping of a Modern Nation* (London: Portobello Books, 2016).

61   Seabrook, John, 'Can a Machine Learn to Write for The New Yorker?', *The New Yorker* (2019), https://www.newyorker.com/magazine/2019/10/14/can-a-machine-learn-to-write-for-the-new-yorker.

62   Epstein, Sophia, 'How Do You Control an AI as Powerful as OpenAI's GPT-3?', *Wired UK* (27 July 2020), https://www.wired.co.uk/article/gpt-3-openai-examples.

63   Hypernormalisation (2016), [documentary] Dir. Adam Curtis, UK: BBC.

64   Pasquale, *The Black Box Society*, 85.

65   Stjernfelt, Frederik and Anne Mette Lauritzen, *Your Post Has Been Removed: Tech Giants and Freedom of Speech* (2020), https://www.springer.com/gp/book/9783030259679, 164.

66   'General Data Protection Regulation (GDPR) – Official Legal Text', https://gdpr-info.eu/

67   Pasquale, *The Black Box Society*, 61.

68   Presner, Todd, 'The Ethics of the Algorithm: Close and Distant Listening to the Shoah Foundation Visual History Archive', in *Probing the Ethics of Holocaust Culture* (Cambridge, 2016), 175–202.

69   Star, 'Power, Technology and the Phenomenology of Conventions: On Being Allergic to Onions', 82.

70 Latour, *Science in Action: How to Follow Scientists and Engineers through Society.*

71 Note: We can find no reference for this study; perhaps it is a sociological myth – or perhaps our keyword search was ineffectual because Google flagged the content we were looking for as too controversial to return a result.

72 Wyse, L., 'Appreciating Machine-Generated Artwork through Deep Learning Mechanisms', in *Big Data – A New Medium?* (Abingdon: Routledge, 2020).

73 For example, Su, Jiawei, Danilo Vasconcellos Vargas and Sakurai Kouichi, 'One Pixel Attack for Fooling Deep Neural Networks', *IEEE Transactions on Evolutionary Computation*, 23/5 (2019), 828–41.

7

Power through datafication

The current deluge of data and the epistemic rupture created by the advent of big data can be termed a 'data revolution'[1] which can be equated with the industrial revolution beginning in the late eighteenth century. The ripples outward from this rupture have been discussed throughout this book. The discourses around big data are often marked by big promises about progress and prosperity driven by technological innovation, the increase in efficiency of scalable businesses and the reduction of their cost, societally beneficial transformations such as open government, transparency and accountability, as well as scientific advances and paradigm shifts. But the creation of data is a costly endeavour. Because they are ultimately a product of human activity and cannot be found 'out there' like a natural resource, one has to recall the whole chain of their production to envision the expenses necessary for their creation: the conceptual work of interpreting the chaos before the eyes of human beings in order to determine what should be identified as 'datum' relevant for a certain purpose and therefore be collected; the work of individuals to either gather data manually (like an archivist writing archival descriptions) or design machines to automatically collect data, both according to the conceptual scheme established earlier; the process of actual data collection, their storage, processing, cleaning, refining, feeding into information infrastructures (which have to be created to begin with) and their wrangling and analysis in order to determine their heuristic value; finally, the societal process of discussing and estimating the truth value of those data. These are the bare minimum steps necessary for the production of data, which involves the cost of human labour as well as the provision of collecting devices, computers, algorithms, storage space and infrastructures.

The result of data being expensive and resource-intensive assets is that 'only already powerful institutions – corporations, governments, and elite research universities – have the means to work with them at scale'.[2] Especially when it comes to the establishment and processing of big data, such institutions are able to raise the cost of workers and technological resources necessary to deal with them. If we truly stand at the beginning of a new epoch in which big data and new data analytics reshape the way business is done, government is exercised, and knowledge is produced, a critical stance will inevitably ask for the implications this data revolution has for power. This goes beyond Zuboff's idea of how companies exploit 'behavioural surplus'[3] and beyond the ability of these actors to make money from human activities; it is about the ability of these same forces to change how we view ourselves, our histories and our identities in the long term.

The tension between the comprehensive promises uttered by the proponents of the new digital age[4] and the voices taking a more critical stance may remind humanists of the debate conducted in the late eighteenth century between the proponents of Enlightenment and Jean-Jacques Rousseau. The latter questioned inequalities and new forms of social injustice introduced by the new era, taking into perspective the sense of exclusion and injury of the underprivileged as well as their resentment against top-down modernization. He was demanding a new 'social contract' by means of which just social conditions as well as a social order based on morals, virtue and human character are central to politics, rather than the gains of commerce and money. Rousseau's critique of the political philosophers focused on their neglect of the negative consequences of the innovations brought about by the revolutions of that time, questioned the pursuit of self-interest as serving civil society, denounced modernity as a system in which power flows to an elite and exposed the use of language to deceive and exploit others as pretension: 'All these great words of society, of justice, of laws, of mutual defence, of assistance to the weak, of philosophy and of the progress of reason are only lures invented by skilful politicians or by flattering cowards to impose them on the simple.'[5] These reflections have been termed 'the autocritique of Enlightenment'.[6]

The nascent digital era and the age of Enlightenment can be compared: while the *philosophes* lived in a time of emerging nation-states, globally acting big tech corporations nowadays assume functions of states. An acknowledged definition of a state describes them as compulsory political organizations with a centralized government maintaining a monopoly of the legitimate use of force. These are elements which can be identified with regard to big tech companies: they determine the rules and restrictions for their users and customers which define the terms of participating in the services provided ('to be naturalized'), and they are hierarchically structured and contain the possibility to be excluded from them ('to be expatriated'). Moreover, the revenues generated by the big tech companies equal the gross domestic product (GDP) of whole nations. Apple, for example, creates yearly revenues which can be compared to the GDP of Vietnam; Amazon's annual sales can be compared to the GDP of Pakistan.[7] Seen against Max Weber's famous definition of a state as 'that human polity which claims for itself (with success) within a certain territory [...] the monopoly of legitimate physical violence',[8] such corporations only lack a territory. Territory is however irrelevant in the digital sphere; for the classic nation-states, it has the function of assets that can be distributed to its citizens and access granted to natural resources. In the digital sphere, data are the complement to natural resources; hence – amongst others – the metaphor of 'data as the new oil' to be exploited. These data are created via the multiplicity of digital devices with their built-in recording and processing functions, the instruments typical for surveillance and governance systems (such as produced by videos or scans as in Google Street view or GPS functionalities built in navigation systems), and by the users and customers themselves (such as through tracking of online activity, transactional data or in the form of the content provided by the users like videos, images and texts).[9] Availability of big data thus puts each big tech company in a position to be 'the superpower that establishes its own values and pursues its own purposes above and beyond the social contracts to which others are bound'.[10]

In taking a critical approach to the discursive regimes around big data and its implications for power relationships, we analysed them as a set of interlocking discourses which justify and support new developments and naturalizes their use. Chapter 2 of this book has analysed the metaphors and terms used for data and data collections, and qualified them as a powerful set of arguments which are euphemistic and revealing with regard to the inequalities and power asymmetries inextricably connected with the distribution of data and thus with the extraction of knowledge and profit. The metaphorization of data as 'natural resources' raises questions about the distribution of the profits gained from their exploitation and towards which end large-scale data are established. Such an investigation opens up the possibility to analyse an extractive system which 'creates a profound asymmetry between who is collecting, storing, and analyzing data, and whose data are collected, stored, and analyzed'.[11] With regard to the latter and in the cultural sphere, state-funded endeavours like the provision of archival descriptions or metadata created by libraries and museums stand in contrast to projects advanced by private companies, like Google Books. In their euphemistic function, the metaphors and terms used for data and data processing conceal the fact that data can be treated as goods with a surplus value, which can be traded and monetized while their markets are 'driven by techniques of "predictive optimization" that attempt to generate future value'.[12] A side effect of the 'naturalization' of data as natural resources is the obfuscation of the status of data as 'always already' epistemically marked by those humans who created the measurement protocols, designed the sensors, and determined their placement and use. Wordings such as 'data warehouse' imply a deprivation from context and suggest that data are to be seen as products without the rich context described in other chapters of this book (which renders them as pre-epistemic and fosters their proposed 'factuality'). As another example, terms like 'artificial neural networks' naturalize information processing by suggesting that activities of predictive modelling can be compared to the functional aspects and structure of the human brain. This metaphor denies that human and computational information processing proceed in entirely different ways; it supports the vision that an understanding of the world as complex as that of a human being can be achieved and excelled by a computer, and that humanity will ultimately be superseded by a superior artificial intelligence equipped with supernatural powers ('singularity'). Finally, even those tasks which cannot be processed by computers are covered behind a figurative term: Amazon's 'Mechanical Turk' recalls the eighteenth-century fake chess-playing machine in which a human chess master was hidden. It appears to accomplish tasks automatically, but in truth makes use of human labour with particularly low wages – another sad example of the exploitation brought about by the data industry – or exploitation that belies the narrative of 'progress' as it did during the industrial revolution.

This chapter focuses on power asymmetries and inequalities introduced in the cultural sector by way of datafication and the exploitation of shared cultural assets by private capital. It sets out to investigate and discuss three areas where these phenomena can be observed and lead to significant disadvantages and marginalizations: language resources, digitized cultural heritage and skewed distributions of data in academia and the private sector. All three areas serve as examples where cultural identities, the extrapolation of knowledge from cultural heritage for the purpose of interpreting history, and the societal functions of the sciences and humanities are set in opposition to the aims and purposes of tech corporations.

Language as data

Language is not only one of the best-developed means of human articulation, but also forms the basis for some of the finest artistic creations of humanity.

Be it in prose, lyric poetry or drama, in philosophical treatises or scientific reflections, cultural and creative expressions make use of language and thus form one of the objects on which the arts and humanities focus. As a connective feature of identity, the use of language links groups of human beings and forms collectives. Since the invention of logics by the Greeks, it has been a dream of humankind to reduce all reasoning to some kind of calculation – a dream that has not been achieved yet, since computers are still poor at truly understanding the complexity of the semantic information contained in any of the languages of the world. While the ambiguity inherent in artistic products bears witness of the wealth of cultural heritage, the transformation of the ambiguous, polysemic, conflicting and contradictory phenomenon of language into data still presents, from a computational view, one of the most thorny challenges to be solved. Language data is in raw form unstructured text, which makes up a sizeable (but by no means dominant) portion of the so-called big data landscape. Ambiguity of human language is a major challenge, both at the lexical level, such as polysemy, and at the syntactic level insofar as sentences formulated in a specific language may not be understood in an unequivocal way.

Major populations in the world either speak English or Mandarin Chinese, with speaker numbers of up to 1.268 billion and 1.120 billion respectively.[13] Since predominant language use entails the provision of large datasets, it is not surprising to find that two of the most often used multilingual neural machine translation services – Google Translate and Baidu Translate – are based in either English- or Mandarin-speaking countries.[14] These circumstances result in power asymmetries and inequalities. First of all, current digital ecosystems are resource-hungry and data-hungry; they need big data. Second, computational power, the application of statistical models and technologies like machine-learning methods (which can be united under the umbrella term 'Artificial Intelligence'), as well as the work of capable developers of algorithms, are necessary for dealing with big data.[15] All these costly ingredients can only be provided by powerful and financially robust institutions. Language as a resource therefore provides an obvious example where big tech companies can be seen as AI Superpowers.

By contrast, in the European Union (EU) there are twenty-four official languages and more than sixty national and regional languages. Many of the latter are spoken by less than half a million speakers, like Breton, Frisian, Icelandic, Irish, Luxembourgish, Maltese and Scots.[16] While for some EU languages like English or Spanish large data volumes are available, it is obvious that the limited coverage of these 'smaller languages' equals data scarcity. For the integration of the EU, on the other hand, the even provision of large volumes of data would be necessary, as this enables machine translation. Machine translation systems need large collections of aligned bilingual text, which are for example provided in parallel corpora such as the Europarl containing the proceedings of the European Parliament in eleven European languages, a resource that wasn't created for the purpose of machine translation. Since language as a resource is context-dependent, data collected in one domain (here parliamentary proceedings or, more commonly, Amazon product reviews) cannot easily be transferred to other domains such as literature, philosophy or film subtitles. Moreover, machine translation is nowadays facilitated by the training of neural networks, which require training data in the magnitude of at least 1 million sentence pairs. Even if there are data in this scale at hand, rare and unseen words won't be translated or have to be complemented manually. These technical requirements have a direct consequence: languages with less than 100,000 speakers do not generate enough data and will therefore not be served by machine translation services. Beyond these data inequalities, the training of neural networks requires powerful hardware with a lot of memory and graphics processing units to parallelize training. Such an infrastructure is costly and can rarely be afforded by small and medium-sized enterprises facilitating machine translation even within the EU, which has been relatively proactive via its policies, funding programmes and research interest groups in promoting machine translation. If these requirements are not fulfilled, the quality of the translation suffers. Moreover, mistakes in input data are exacerbated by neural machine translation systems which are sensitive to faulty data.[17] Data issues – such as errors, noise and inconsistencies in coverage – therefore have a crucial impact on the quality of the services. Furthermore, frequently encountered issues with language resources pertain to the openness of available data – especially where corporations own large volumes of data[18] – as well as Intellectual Property Rights, for example, with digitally available texts in small languages. The unequal availability of language data disadvantages and marginalizes smaller languages, since 'machine learning is only as intelligent as the amount of data it has to train on',[19] and it causes power asymmetries with regard to the companies providing translation services: 'No LT [language technology] company in Europe is even of comparable size to the big players like Google or Baidu.'[20] The fact that large amounts of data are available in some languages while others are only represented by a little also results in a Matthew effect[21] created by ownership: larger corporations have access to large volumes of data, while smaller companies are left behind. While larger corporations are able to extend their services and their quality, smaller companies won't be able to close the gap in terms of data, hardware and software and will become economically inefficient. In this way, language data is making the big bigger and the small smaller. Smaller languages suffer from the Matthew effect as well: due to their limited size, they are regarded as being susceptible to be deviant from the default, as infrequent use is translated into minimal predictions of use.

As the example of the EU shows, data inequalities have direct consequences not only for companies providing machine translation services, but for the economy in general – and for citizenship. Customers ordering online prefer webshops where information on the products is provided in their native language. In a competitive environment, companies must focus on maximizing their profits; 'the affordability of language technologies is […] a problem for SMEs that want to translate their online services and cannot assume the cost of doing so'.[22] Within Europe as a multilingual market, data scarcity thus presents a major impediment for business across language. Businesses that cannot provide content in local languages may therefore become economic losers, and the uneven distribution of language data may lead to fragmented markets. Moreover, for European citizens, multilingualism presents a key feature of Europeanness. While it may be possible to translate in a concerted effort all documents necessary for administration within the EU (e.g. to ensure mobility and the free exercise of a profession within the EU), constraints in the provision of translation services directly affect participation in the political process. To provide but one example: 'Following the Fukushima incident in 2011 there have been discussions about the dangers of nuclear energy in all European countries. These debates were held in the respective language communities only, there has never been a public European debate about the topic because it is, technically, not yet possible to organize such a debate online'.[23] Within the EU, the lack of language resources and technologies may therefore limit citizens' engagement in collective debates, the development of cross-border solutions and their participation in decision-making processes. Fostering a common European identity while maintaining the cultural and linguistic diversity of Europe therefore presents a substantial challenge. Whereas the officially acknowledged languages of the EU are granted – at least in principle – equal status, it will take a large-scale effort to enable the use of high-quality language technologies by balancing the asymmetries inherent in the available data for all European languages. Within the multilingual landscape of Europe, the mutual recognition of the diversity of linguistic origins and traditions forms a cornerstone of the development of a common European identity.

Cultural heritage

The shift from analogue finding aids to digital archival descriptions provided by cultural heritage institutions (CHIs) has been thoroughly explored in preceding chapters. It is useful to revisit this frame of reference once more, however, as this movement can also be understood in terms of Erving Goffman's 'breach and repair' approach, in that cultural heritage 'practitioners' reactions to the disruption of their practice offer the opportunity to glimpse the norms of archival thinking'.[24] The digitization of archival material and the provision of digitally available descriptions have consequences for the relationships between cultural heritage practitioners and users/researchers and accordingly practitioners and technicians on the one hand, and for the power structures regarding access to knowledge and knowledge creation on the other hand.

The relationship between cultural heritage practitioners (such as archivists) and the users of CHIs has changed profoundly. While more and more archival descriptions have become available in electronic formats – the Archives Portal Europe currently provides 283,774,614 descriptive units of archives[25] – it is still the case that archivists function as the gatekeepers to cultural heritage and, as the experts for the material they preside over, provide the first entry points to it. As the interviews we conducted reveal, archivists assume that a direct and dialogic relationship with users is and will be maintained. As one librarian stated:

> And our descriptions here are very, very detailed. For example, I have a manuscript here and I'm describing it. I look through it. [...] But at the end, you know the whole thing. It helps us very much when we have to answer requests. Because on one side you can find all that data in our database, and on the other side, even if there are some technical [reasons a user] can't find it, we can find it.
>
> (WP3 INT1)

But the findability of archival descriptions online also promotes the possibility that users avoid a direct exchange with an archivist or deem it to be superfluous, thus cutting archivists off from their function as gatekeepers to cultural heritage. Furthermore, as cultural heritage practitioners learn the language of technology, a power shift towards the technical personnel takes place in these institutions. 'Practitioners' experiences of the power dynamics at play when other specialists enter heritage spaces suggest that their perspective is the unique contribution most at risk of being squeezed out of the discourse.'[26] It is obvious that sound personal relationships and mutual recognition become essential in order to avoid power asymmetries within CHIs.

While the establishment of trusted relationships between practitioners and users is changing during the transitional phase of digitization, the establishment of digital archival descriptions pre-forms the way in which meaning and knowledge are created. Archivists themselves notice their own detachment from the material they presided over, as they

> are not working on item level anymore, you are trying to subtract the general meaning, the general line from a collection [...] For every new collection that comes in, you can't go in depth, reading every page in detail, you skim through and you seek the major subject. We're not as close to the items anymore.
>
> (WP3 INT3)

Cultural heritage practitioners must decide how to describe an item or collection and to place more emphasis on including the context of the item or on the connections with other items or collections. They do not have the resources to transfer their tacit knowledge to the systems with which they must work.

> We decided not to make a characteristic description of the pictures. That means that we only give the original caption of the photograph. [...] These are propaganda captions, in fact, because these pictures were taken during the war by specific agencies ... that is why we decided to transcribe the original caption, but without giving any other information. And also, because we don't have time, we don't have staff to describe individually each picture, so we inventorised pictures with a thematic logic.
>
> (WP3 INT4)

In this example, presenting the original context of the holdings was prioritized over making connections with other collections. In a wider sense, the anticipated future uses of these archival descriptions therefore elevate one meaning above the exploration of complex alternatives.

Many archives are still in a transitional period where only a fraction of their holdings descriptions are available online, while the archival material itself still requires a visit to the archive: 'You can access only the part of the documents that are tagged that it's okay to be online. It's a pyramid on the website, you will have only a small part of the description and the documents. In the reading room, you will have this box in addition' (WP3 INT2). The material presented online currently presents only a small fraction, with clear implications for the material buried at deeper levels of accessibility. A decision to choose one collection for digitization and online access over another therefore privileges that knowledge directly in that it increases its chances of being studied by researchers, as has been explicated in Chapter 5. With regard to an automated analysis of digitized historical sources during the transitional period we are currently in, such a partial approach to digital discoverability and the exploitation of the data provided online would exclude those sources which have not been and will never be digitized or contained in archival descriptions, and such analyses would render at best a distorted knowledge of our shared past.

As has been discussed in Chapter 5, cultural heritage practitioners have already observed the formation of search habits on the side of the users, who imitate the keyword-search approach to knowledge established by Google, thereby simplifying their access to complexity and losing sight of what might not be available in digital format. Cultural heritage practitioners are moreover well aware of their lack of experience in what could be done with the collection descriptions by means of aggregation:

> Data-linking is one of the limitations we have to take into account, and it's one of the primary factors in terms of restricting data, because even if you've removed all the direct identifiers, maybe indirect information that could be used to identify them, even something that seems innocuous like the type of building material used in a house could, in some cases, be used to identify the specific house in a region because they use certain types of material ... and the identifiers that are used, even if they're a numeric ID, could be linked to an existing dataset. It could be linked to the personal data that people have stored elsewhere than they're supposed to.
>
> (WP3 INT5)

Such data aggregation could, for example, be performed by institutions or companies which have the means to establish large databases of citation networks, which could then be aligned with archival descriptions containing anonymized information on persons and their written exchanges with other historical personalities, thus enabling de-anonymization. In the interviews conducted within the KPLEX project, archivists proved to be well aware of the fact that the digital material they expose becomes vulnerable to misuse:

> Certainly, the machine processing is, I suppose, going to be even bigger soon than it is now, and [...] artificial intelligence has the potential to draw new conclusions from a large amount of data, particularly unstructured data, which [...] until quite recent years have resisted the broader analysis [...] if automated tools are able to make links between those datasets and then [...] infer conclusions about the people, if it's identified, then there's a significant danger to them.
>
> (WP3 INT5)

Research methods may become increasingly mediated by automated tools through which machine learning algorithms will play an increased role not only in analysis but also in discoverability through linked data. Currently, cultural heritage practitioners mediate as gatekeepers of material that is vulnerable to misuse. However, online discoverability and access to digital data may expose a dark side, where potential threats are magnified beyond those that can be seen unaided, by the use of AI and big data tools. It is as yet unclear to which results such automated data analyses will lead, but certainly only a few researchers and institutions are capable of capitalizing on big data on cultural heritage and exploiting the possibilities that lie therein. Whereas the capacity of historians to process large amounts of information is limited (the case of which presents a well-documented and understood confirmation bias), information processing performed by computers can be scaled to enormous quantities of available data. The interpretation of cultural heritage is a complex process endangered by the threat that some forms of knowledge will not properly be translated by computational methods.

Take the development of dominant patterns of thought as an example: while it would be absolutely interesting to investigate the evolution of such concepts like racism or empathy over the course of several centuries and on the basis of large collections of data, it has to be questioned whether such information can adequately be treated by machines incapable of navigating the ambivalences and polysemies inherent in the data which are analysed, since they would have to be able to appropriately place such data in their historical context and consider the shifts and caesuras characteristic of historical development. For example, the encounter of Columbus and his men with the indigenous people they met during their 'discovery' of the Americas can be understood according to the attitudes prevailing in the context of their time; it would form a completely different approach to interpret them in terms of the paradigms of racism and empathy which have been developed centuries later. Historical knowledge is always situated knowledge insofar as it is itself placed in time and assesses and revaluates past events from a certain point of view. It follows then that power shifts or revolutions result in shifts in the interpretation of history, as has happened, for example, after the end of the cold war and the fall of the iron curtain or during the phase of decolonization. After such caesuras, a reinterpretation and revaluation of historical events take place which exploit the ambivalences and polysemies typical for historical sources.

Seen against this background, it is highly questionable whether research results achieved by computational means will ever be capable of providing insights adequate to the historical record beyond such highly formalized data collections and processing methods like social network analysis. Furthermore, processes like identity formation and the provision of answers as to how a collective's identity or sense of belonging to one state or one nation arises do not rely on historical evidence in a self-evident way, as the well-researched examples of invented traditions and imagined communities show.[27] The rewriting of the grand narratives and foundational myths of nations has repeatedly taken place, embedded into complex processes like the emergence of nation-states or the fall of empires, and they are themselves part of societal processes and large-scale discursive shifts in which the community of historians is in constant exchange with each other in order to adjust their insights and epistemics with the society in which they live and whose questions they are supposed to answer. It is precisely this knowledge of context and this experience of being-in-a-situation which separates the work of a historian from that of machine intelligence, which always must begin at the level of objectivity and rationality where the facts have already been produced and the data are already at hand. The question is therefore what the power shift currently on the horizon with regard to knowledge creation in the realm of cultural heritage will look like. With regard to the power structures at stake here, the tension between knowledge creation processes performed by government-financed historians and private data analysis laboratories owned by tech corporations is crucial. This tension pertains to questions of the legitimate production of knowledge, the credibility accounted to the results[28] and the mechanisms of producing expert consensus in scientific communities.[29]

The academic field

'Knowledge is power', according to Sir Francis Bacon. Even though data are not powerful in and of themselves, scientific disciplines realize meaning and value from data; control over data therefore also introduces asymmetries into the academic field, as we were able to observe within the KPLEX project in our study of the research topic 'emotions', in which we analysed data collection, production, differing methodological epistemic cultures and research organization in a broad range of scientific disciplines.[30] In the field of academic emotion research, such asymmetries can best be illustrated by juxtaposing the experimental approach applied by neuroscience and research conducted in the field by anthropologists. Neuroscience has built a huge research structure in order to explore research participants' individual emotional responses to the stimuli presented in a fMRI scanner. This research setting includes the maintenance of an expensive laboratory designed for this specific purpose, as well as the provision of specialized technical personnel and administrative staff. The output of the costly machinery amounts to several gigabytes of data per research participant. On the other side of the disciplinary spectrum, anthropological emotion research represents a quite different methodological approach: a solitary ethnographer conducts research within a culture that is initially alien to the researcher and may confront her with overwhelming complexity. Here subjectivities and relationality come into play, elements that are (supposedly) missing in the technical environments of controlled experiments. The output in terms of data consists of the field notes taken by the researcher, dialogues conducted during the field trip, analyses reflecting the positionality of the researcher and so on. The contrast between laboratory and field thus illuminates the extreme poles of differing 'epistemic cultures'[31] at play in emotion research.

The availability of large datasets in the academic field necessitates employing data scientists alongside the subject matter experts. This division of labour inevitably produces a power shift with regard to the question as to who is the most legitimate producer of knowledge – the domain expert or the statistician analysing the data. Interdisciplinary research settings create their own difficulties of organizing research in larger research units and influence the relationships established between disciplines and researchers: 'So interdisciplinarity [...] always comes with dependencies in a way, between the people, new dependencies, and so you have again power relations within an interdisciplinary project that are different to purely disciplinary projects' (WP4 INT12). Such circumstances may impose structural limitations on the research project insofar as they lead to conflicts and debates about the methodological approach within the research team, as one researcher reported:

> And to me one of the kind of biggest lessons learned during this project was that being a humanities social science person and starting to work with quantitative people. I thought that quantitative people are kind of the same (laughing). You know, I thought that statistics people and natural language processing and machine learning that they kind of agree. But there's huge differences between them. So, the first year was basically/I thought that the big divide would be me with them or us with them. But it ended up that they among themselves were fighting. Like really fighting because statistics people, for instance, socially, their data was problematic in MANY, many ways because they didn't know where it came from. So, actually their ideas aligned very well with my ideas that we need to do some sort of ethnography around the production of the data.
>
> (WP4 INT11)

Another of our interviewees reported from the experiences made within a larger research unit where neuroscientists collaborated with social scientists and humanists. Since each discipline brought their own epistemic approach as well as requirements as to knowledge complexity and differentiation of results, each discipline searched for legitimacy, recognition and autonomy which resulted in a competitive struggle within the academic field and brought the tensions created by asymmetric power distributions and monopolies to the surface. In the example of emotion research, the tensions arose between the limitations imposed by the use of a fMRI scanner, the output of which is measured according the variables of valence and arousal, and the complex and differentiated conceptions of human emotions characteristic of the social sciences and humanities:

> In this cluster I worked together with a psychologist, a developmental psychologist. But now: no [more]. [...] And this was a deliberate decision. Because especially during this [...] big excellence cluster we reach the/I would say we came to our limits. And this has to do with research methodologies. And so, one problem was, or an example with persons like [...], he's also a brain researcher. And he was very open-minded and very interested in our kind of work. And we spend hours and hours and nights together and conceptualised very complex projects. And he said: 'You are so right, this is so important, but we cannot do this. We have this brain scanner. And it's too complex. We have to design a common project with two variables.' To be able to/that it fits into this scan thing. This was the end of [...] collaboration. I said: 'It's, sorry, but it's too stupid for us. I cannot do it!' Yeah, it's [...] in my own discipline. If I reduce this complexity to these two things you can see in your scan. [...] And we all made this experience and said: 'So, it's enough!'
>
> (WP4 INT15)

As the example shows, the multiplicity of epistemic approaches within a single large research endeavour fostered the entrenchment of academic disciplines from each other and contributed to mutually exclusive approaches within the ivory tower. Most interestingly, the cessation of interdisciplinary collaboration within emotion research resulted out of the lack of differentiation possible within the large datasets provided by a fMRI scanner:

> My own thought on this has been: How can neuroscientists do these brain scans and not consider that the person that they are scanning is an individual person with a biography and cultural embeddedness and that sort of thing? You are not looking at a brain; you are looking at someone's brain! You can aggregate, I suppose, lots of data from a lot of different peoples' brains and arrive at some

sort of average, you know, values, but still you are dealing with brains that are embedded in a certain time and space and society and you should take account of that. But neuroscientists cannot and do not want to. [...] what I would really like to see is the effects of practice on the brain. From the perspective of practice theory there is an assumption that doing something over and over does in fact change the body, the physical body.

(WP4 INT6)

The uneven distribution of data does not only pertain to processes of distinction between academic disciplines; when asked about big data in a conventional sense, cultural heritage professionals proved to be quite critical about the strategies employed by big tech companies, where data are collected and processed by specially designed research units. They underlined here that the commercial aims pursued with the aggregation of big data fundamentally differ from academic research purposes.

Just gathering data because you can is something not very reasonable for me, right? And many of the big data sets, for example service providers have or Google has might be usable for specific reasons, the purchase behaviour of people or whatever, but it is not desirable for me if I want to pursue my own research which is then the speech related data. [...] So, the big data is a different kind of data, data types, right? But of course, these companies or entities, organizations also, they have a big advantage if they have the access to this kind of data. [...] They also are very active in research, but not necessarily with externalising all of the data, right? But with participating in the knowledge exploration, basically in the scientific process, yes, but not really sharing the data.

(WP4 INT5)

The competition between economic enterprises controlling big data and the academic field results in a terminological differentiation between on the one hand very large datasets (such as video collections or aggregated fMRI data from the neurosciences) that were termed 'research data', because they were conceived according to an elaborated epistemology and methodology and collected guided by scientific reasoning; and 'big data' on the other hand, a term designating data that were not collected for specific research purposes and thus regarded to be antecedent to the epistemological process on the other hand. The reflections and comments uttered by scientific researchers reflected the debate initiated by the article on the 'end of theory' published by Chris Anderson,[32] but focused on the implicit epistemological assumptions with regard to research driven by big data, rather than an overt discussion of questions of power, legitimacy or financial support. The claim that there is no need for a priori theory was criticized as an unscientific approach, since specific research questions within a determined research framework were seen to be essential for a steered, methodologically controlled research process, which was contrasted with an investigation conducted in an exploratory manner open for serendipitous findings:

> I mean this is the big game of big data, of how you/or why everyone who says I do big data speaks of it and gets money and stuff, because it's a very cheap way to correlate datasets and then find new things. But the question remains – if you don't have a question then why do you look for an answer?
>
> (WP4 INT12)

The idea that big data can speak for themselves free of human bias was regarded as misleading, insofar as such a claim ignores the design of data collection tools and the values, assumptions, biases and interests driving the design process. Moreover, a humanistic approach was outlined that called for a balanced approach to biases in big data:

> There is a group of researchers who are kind of like: big data is objective, or it gives us objective views to the world. And of course, we all know that that's not the case. [...] And I think the interventions that we can do is to demonstrate that there are so many different ways of understanding what is knowledge. What's the truth value of knowledge? Where it's coming from? How there're always biases. And we have to acknowledge them. That sometimes human bias is a very good thing. You know, we come from a country with a lot of gender politics. That's mostly a bias. But we think that this is an important bias to take gender into account and sometimes favour women. Or sometimes favour minorities. So, these are like human biases that are needed for society building and advancement.
>
> (WP4 INT11)

Finally, the claim that big data strives for exhaustivity and enables one to see everything within a specific domain was directly contradicted in our interviews, which is not surprising since this claim, when applied to the academic field, calls the idea of a differentiation into several specialized scientific disciplines into question. With regard to big data collected online, one researcher remarked that such data may allow knowledge creation about human behaviour, but does not provide insight into motivation and emotion:

So, for example there is, within big data there is a lot of behavioural tracking. And I go back to booking.com example, so they are definitely doing big data analysis. And what they're doing is […] they answer the question: What do I have to do in order to make the most profit out of the website? And for that their approach is pretty much optimal […]. If their question would be: What does make my customers feel the best? Then their type of research probably wouldn't be as good as comparable methods within neuroscience for example or […] qualitative research just asking the users in-depth-interviews or something like that. Because with the behavioural data you don't get any information about how they feel. You just get information of whether they stick on the website or whether they move away from it.

(WP4 INT13)

This line of argumentation echoes on the one hand the dispute about the representativity of data which were collected only online versus those data collected with social sciences methods (surveys, public-opinion polls);[33] on the other hand, it points to the discursive tensions elicited by the suggestive and powerful set of arguments brought forward in the discussion triggered by Chris Anderson's article, which can be described as a discursive regime in Foucault's sense. Moreover, the competition between academia and tech giants holding big data comes into view: the academics interviewed in the KPLEX project expressed their dismay that the production of knowledge from big data occurs unmoored from science. Research fields that are claimed to be traditionally a part of academic endeavours (such as questions pertaining to whole populations and to the characteristics of society) come into opposition with the explanatory power proposed to be derivable from big data and the claims to representativeness driven by business interests. Moreover, the balance of knowledge creation in society becomes destabilized in favour of the big tech companies: 'This unprecedented concentration of knowledge produces an equally unprecedented concentration of power: asymmetries that must be understood as the *unauthorized privatization of the division of learning in society.*'[34] In other words, the creation of knowledge out of big data beyond academia and the skewed distribution of data between scientific and business institutions results in power struggles between these two autonomous institutions about the legitimacy of providing answers to societally relevant questions, as well as about their relationship to the third major institution holding big datasets, namely governments.

Conclusion

Language data, digitized cultural heritage and academic endeavours are but three examples of fields where power asymmetries and inequalities can be observed and brought into dialogue with those discourses of power over big data, computing capacity, statistical models and technologies, and algorithm experts exerted by the big tech companies. If we recall the reflections brought forward by Jean-Jacques Rousseau with respect to the Enlightenment's vision of the new era to come and his discussion of the sources of inequalities (competence, ownership, wealth creating and directing new needs), and if we apply these reflections to the new digital era to come, we must discuss the consequences of these asymmetries and inequalities for society. While governments are slow in establishing data infrastructures and providing analytic possibilities for their citizens, and while academia is restricted by the various interests which drive research forward, big tech corporations exert power on their users and customers while they silently exploit the data collectively contributed by them for the purposes of private corporations. The power of these companies rests on the exploitation of volunteered data (such as in the case of Wikipedia or the Open Street Map), in the form of data provided as content, expertise, opinions and knowledge (such as through data created in social media, in applications quantifying the self, on crowdsourcing platforms, or in citizen science), and in cultural heritage data in general (such as in the printed books digitized by Google Books).[35] This authority is exerted in an opaque, algorithmically implemented way, as in the manipulation of opinions via social media, which stands in contrast to free opinion formation, in the direction of consumers' choices via search engines and the creation of needs through recommendation systems, and, generally, in behaviour modification, since 'automated machine processes not only *know* our behavior but also *shape* our behavior at scale'.[36]

But the notion that big tech corporations can be compared to states opens up the question of whether users and consumers and the data they contribute should rightly be granted the revenues enjoyed by such global corporations. Instead of reducing human beings to users and consumers, they should rather be regarded as citizens endowed with political rights which are suitable 'to protect their liberty, and not to enslave them',[37] and who can actively participate in the spread of the revenues gained and profit from the benefits achieved. Following the example of Rousseau, we can observe that the big tech companies turn shared cultural assets – be it in the form of collectively created large language data, in the form of cultural heritage which can be regarded as cultural commons or those data forming the basis of knowledge creation – into corporate capital. This observation reveals the differences between private corporations and nation-states: cultural heritage represents a public good, and opinions and aesthetic choices contributed via social media, crowdsourced platforms or recommender systems should be regarded as cultural commons as well.

Rather than serving as a resource to be exploited by tech giants – like the labour provided by a Mechanical Turk – and thus encouraging the cultural colonialism of private corporations, such big data should be treated as public commodities. This presents a tricky challenge for regulation and an issue for antitrust laws, since markets can be assumed to exist even if the services provided by corporations are free of charge, for example, in the case where users pay with their data: 'The problem for regulators is that standard anti-monopoly frameworks do not apply in a world where the costs to consumers (mainly in the form of data and privacy) are thoroughly non-transparent.'[38] But these markets have two layers, the first one being the commons which have a societal value, and the second one formed by these commons being datafied, which enables corporations to skim their economic value. The idea of cultural commons therefore needs to be revitalized and reformulated with respect to the monetary value of data, where free access to such big data is granted in order to provide the possibility to realize the chances and opportunities which lie therein for the common good. Free access to such data could either take the form of a 'data-sharing mandate',[39] or data should stay in public ownership just as non-digital cultural commons. Google Books serves as a good example here, since technically no objection can be raised against a corporation claiming to have digitized 40 million books[40] as long as all the content is openly accessible. But Google Books is a revenue-generating project and not a library.[41] Libraries, by contrast, are funded by the public sector and provide their data, metadata schemes and APIs openly to everybody interested in using such services. As this example shows, data need to be understood as an essential part of infrastructures, which should be owned by the public just as artificial intelligence built on top of them; conceptualized in this way, data would form public commodities which can be used by several agents simultaneously, but private corporations would have to pay for their use.[42] In the sense of Rousseau, such a reformulation of the idea of cultural commons would level out inequalities and forms of social injustice brought about by the current data revolution and constitute a new social contract with the full participation of citizens as members of a polity.

Notes

1   Kitchin, Rob, *The Data Revolution: Big Data, Open Data, Data Infrastructures and Their Consequences* (London: Sage, 2014).

2   D'Ignazio, Catherine and Lauren F. Klein, *Data Feminism* (Cambridge, MA/London: MIT Press, 2020), 41.

3   Zuboff, Shoshana, *The Age of Surveillance Capitalism* (London: Profile, 2019), 74.

4   See here for example the publications by Bostrom, Nick, *Superintelligence. Paths, Dangers, Strategies* (Oxford: Oxford University Press, 2014); Brynjolfsson, Erik and Andrew McAfee, *The Second Machine Age. Work, Progress, and Prosperity in a Time of Brilliant Technologies* (New York: W. W. Norton & Company Inc, 2014); Tegmark, Max, *Life 3.0. Being Human in the Age of Artificial Intelligence* (London: Allen Lane, 2017).

5   Rousseau, Jean-Jacques, *Œuvres Complètes (Fragments Politiques)* (Paris: Pléiade, 1964), 475, own translation.

6   Hulliung, Mark, *The Autocritique of Enlightenment: Rousseau and the Philosophes* (Cambridge, MA: Harvard University Press, 1994).

7   Numbers were provided in July 2020: Daly, Kyle, '4 Numbers That Show the Combined Power of Facebook, Google, Apple and Amazon', *Axios*, https://www.axios.com/big-techs-power-in-4-numbers-de8a5bc3-65b6-4064-a7cb-3466c68b2ea0.html.

8   Weber, Max, *Wirtschaft und Gesellschaft: Grundriß der verstehenden Soziologie*, 5th edn (Tübingen: J.C.B. Mohr (Paul Siebeck), 1980), 822, own translation. Compare here: Hay, Colin, *Routledge Encyclopedia of International Political Economy* (New York: Routledge, 2001), 1469–74. Lesser-known alternative definitions of states do without the notion of territory by focusing on the functions of states with regard to sovereignty, welfare and security. See Lehmkuhl, Ursula and Thomas Risse, *Regieren ohne Staat? Governance in Räumen begrenzter Staatlichkeit* (Baden-Baden: Nomos, 2007), 2–10.

9   Kitchin, *The Data Revolution: Big Data, Open Data, Data Infrastructures and Their Consequences*, 87–98.

10 Zuboff, *The Age of Surveillance Capitalism*, 82.

11 D'Ignazio and Klein, *Data Feminism*, 45.

12 Raley, R., 'Dataveillance and Counterveillance', in *'Raw Data' Is an Oxymoron* (Cambridge, MA: MIT Press, 2013), 124.

13 'List of Languages by Total Number of Speakers', *Wikipedia* (2021), https://en.wikipedia.org/w/index.php?title=List_of_languages_by_total_number_of_speakers&oldid=1006949475.

14 Google Translate supports translation between 108 languages, with 100 billion words translated per day. The most common translations are between English and

Spanish, Arabic, Russian, Portuguese and Indonesian. See 'Ten Years of Google
Translate', *Google* (2016), https://blog.google/products/translate/ten-years-of-
google-translate/; 'Google Translate Adds Five Languages', *Google*, 2020, https://
blog.google/products/translate/five-new-languages/.
Baidu Translate supports translation between 203 languages, with 100 billion
characters (in modern Chinese, most words are compounds written with two or
more characters) translated per day. The most common translations are between
Mandarin Chinese and English, Japanese, Korean, Spanish, Thai, French and
Arabic. See Baidu Research, *Twitter* (2020), https://twitter.com/baiduresearch/
status/1248316242689019904; '百度百科', https://vhsagj.smartapps.baidu.com/
pages/lemma/lemma?lemmaTitle=%E7%99%BE%E5%BA%A6%E7%BF%BB%E
8%AF%91&lemmaId=10607809&from=bottomBarShare&hostname=baiduboxa
pp&_swebfr=1.

15 Lee, Kai-Fu, *AI Superpowers. China, Silicon Valley, and the New World Order*
(Boston: Houghton Mifflin Harcourt, 2018), 14.

16 See the report: European Parliament. Directorate General for Parliamentary
Research Services. *Language Equality in the Digital Age: Towards a
Human Language Project* (Brussels: STOA, 2017), https://data.europa.eu/
doi/10.2861/136527.

17 Edmond, Jennifer, Rihards Kalnins, Andrejs Vasiljevs and Mārcis Pinnis, 'KPLEX
Report on Language and Culture as Data' (2018), https://easy.dans.knaw.nl/ui/
datasets/id/easy-dataset:114127.

18 Google, for example, uses the texts scanned by the Google Books project for
machine translation purposes.

19 Zuboff, *The Age of Surveillance Capitalism*, 188.

20 SRIA Editorial Team, *Language Technologies for Multilingual Europe – Towards a
Human Language Project* (2017), http://www.cracking-the-language-barrier.eu/wp-
content/uploads/SRIA-V1.0-final.pdf, 13.

21 Merton, Robert K., 'The Matthew Effect in Science', *Science*, 159/3810 (1968), 56–63.

22 European Parliament. Directorate General for Parliamentary Research Services.
Language Equality in the Digital Age: Towards a Human Language Project, 38.

23 Language Technologies for Multilingual Europe – Towards a Human Language
Project, 24.

24 Horsley, Nicola, 'Intellectual Autonomy after Artificial Intelligence: The Future
of Memory Institutions and Historical Research', in *Big Data – A New Medium?*
(Abingdon: Routledge, 2020), 130–44.

25 'Archives Portal Europe', https://www.archivesportaleurope.net/home.

26 Edmond, Jennifer, Mike Priddy and Nicola Horsley, 'KPLEX Report on
Historical Data as Sources' (2018), https://easy.dans.knaw.nl/ui/datasets/id/easy-
dataset:114127, 77.

27 Anderson, Benedict, *Imagined Communities: Reflections on the Origin and Spread of Nationalism* (London: Verso, 1991); Hobsbawm, Eric and Terence Ranger, *The Invention of Tradition* (Cambridge, UK: Cambridge University Press, 1983).

28 Haraway, Donna, 'Modest Witness: Feminist Diffractions in Science Studies', in *The Disunity of Science. Boundaries, Contexts, Power* (Stanford, CA: Stanford University Press), 432.

29 Oreskes, Naomi, *Why Trust Science?* (Princeton: Princeton University Press, 2019), 57.

30 Edmond, Jennifer, Thomas Stodulka, Elisabeth Huber and Jörg Lehmann, 'KPLEX Report on Data, Knowledge Organization and Epistemics' (2018), https://easy.dans. knaw.nl/ui/datasets/id/easy-dataset:114127.

31 Knorr-Cetina, Karin, *Epistemic Cultures: How the Sciences Make Knowledge* (Cambridge, MA: Harvard University Press, 1999).

32 Anderson, Chris, 'The End of Theory: The Data Deluge Makes the Scientific Method Obsolete', *Wired* (2008), https://www.wired.com/2008/06/pb-theory/. For a thorough discussion of the fallacies inherent in basic assumptions with regard to big data, see Kitchin, *The Data Revolution: Big Data, Open Data, Data Infrastructures and Their Consequences*, 133–7.

33 See, for example, the debate conducted in Germany between the two public opinion poll institutes Forsa and Civey, the latter of which does collect its data only online; compare here: Pausch, Robert and Fritz Zimmermann, 'Umfrageinstitute: Kampf Der Torten', *ZEIT ONLINE* (2020), https://www.zeit.de/2020/07/umfrageinstitute-meinungsforscher-sozialforschung-civey-forsa.

34 Zuboff, *The Age of Surveillance Capitalism*, 192. Original emphasis.

35 Google estimated in 2010 that there were about 130 million distinct titles in the world; see Jackson, Joab, 'Google: 129 Million Different Books Have Been Published', *PC World*, https://www.pcworld.com/article/202803/google_129_million_different_books_have_been_published.html, and it stated that it intended to scan all of them. As of October 2019, Google celebrated fifteen years of Google Books and provided the number of scanned books as more than 40 million titles in over 400 languages; see Google, '15 Years of Google Books', 2019, https://www.blog. google/products/search/15-years-google-books/.

36 Zuboff, *The Age of Surveillance Capitalism*, 8.

37 Rousseau, Jean-Jacques, *The Social Contract and Discourses* (London and Toronto: J.M. Dent and Sons, 1913), https://oll.libertyfund.org/title/cole-the-social-contract-and-discourses.

38 Rogoff, Kenneth, 'Big Tech Is a Big Problem', *Project Syndicate* (2018), https://www. project-syndicate.org/commentary/regulating-big-tech-companies-by-kenneth-rogoff-2018-07?barrier=accesspaylog.

39 Mayer-Schönberger, Victor and Thomas Ramge, *Reinventing Capitalism in the Age of Big Data* (London: John Murray, 2018), 167.

40 Google, '15 Years of Google Books' (2019), https://www.blog.google/products/search/15-years-google-books/.

41 Vaidhyanathan, Siva, *The Googlization of Everything (and Why We Should Worry)*, (Berkeley: The University of California Press, 2012), 149–73.

42 Morozov, Evgeny, 'Socialize the Data Centres!', *New Left Review*, 91 (2015), https://newleftreview.org/II/91/evgeny-morozov-socialize-the-data-centres, 45–66.

8

Expatriates in the land of data: Software tensions as a clash of culture

More questions than answers?

The preceding chapters have presented myriad examples and evidence of the tensions that result from the intersection between common cultural practices and datafication's whispered promises of progressing the efficiency and connection for which we depend upon them. We have shown how power relations are being rebuilt according to the voices that get heard and the capital that is accumulated via 'surveillance capitalism'.[1] We have shown how histories (or perhaps futures) become rewritten, and how identities can be shaped by overarching imaginaries, like the nation states of old. We have explored the promises of knowledge creation paradigms based upon big data and shown how words we think we understand come to accrete rich new fields of meaning that short circuit rather than facilitate mutual understanding. We have shown how trusted institutions, from legal contracts to library collections, become divorced from the values and purposes they have traditionally held.

The discussion throughout this book allows us to reframe questions of the future development of technologies based on big data away from the very narrow issues such as data protection and the prevention of direct abuse towards questions that are far more holistic and centred of the human experience, such as:

§ *Do current data regulation platforms go far enough, and should algorithms be regulated?*

§ *How can the needs of the wider society be taken into account within an ecosystem in which software is generally designed to meet the needs of a client or a user?*

§ *How can the tension between what a client wants to see and the requirements for decision making be resolved against a backdrop of software as a product which needs to be user friendly, to be competitive?*

§ *How can the tendency of those currently wielding power over and through the digital to consolidate access, power and wealth be shifted towards a more equitable, redistributed benefit? As data inequality emerges as a major theme in data-driven society, what are the consequences of this inequality in terms of technology, infrastructure and employment?*

§ *Is there a potential to facilitate redistribution between the data-rich and data-poor and other kinds of economic inequality?*

§ *How do our digital practices evidence the gendered, classed and racialized bias that are relayed via everyday practices and exclusions?*

§ *How are hierarchies and everyday discrimination being sublimated into our data and platforms, how do the implications of this process infringe upon human dignity and diversity, and how can big data systems empower rather than marginalize under these conditions?*

§ *What does 'narrative' mean within the context of the data-focused computer sciences, and how does this tacit definition effect human sensemaking in the digital age?*

§ *The relationship between narrative and data has received much attention from philosophers of science, being variously presented as antagonistic, antithetical or even symbiotic; existing in relationships that can pose ethical and epistemological challenges for the researcher or software engineer. Less has been said about how this relationship is perceived within the computer science community. How can one make data comprehensible if you define it a priori as patternless, objective input?*

§ *How does the human need to make sense through storytelling become recast in an era that seems to fetishize data as having an almost god-like claim to truth?*

§ *With the growing push for Government regulation of AI, the 'Driverless Dilemma' has emerged as a uniquely computational development on the well-established 'trolley problem' wherein a driverless car must choose between the lesser of two evils. Rather than asking whether it is possible to design something that can make machines more humane, should we consider whether it is possible to design machines that make people more humane?*

§ *If human happiness requires human agency, why therefore are we so concerned about machines either taking on human characteristics (such as creativity or imagination) or not having them (like ethics)?*

§ *Why has complexity become coterminous with stress and frustration, or viewed as a risk to be managed?*

§ *How do we invest trust and delegate decision making to algorithms when we do not understand fully how they function (e.g. black box, deep learning) or know what it means to 'trust' a machine?*

§ *Do we believe that the decomposition of complex tasks into executable subroutines perhaps changes the nature of both the question and the answer (or do we care)?*

§ *If we accept the proposition that attention should be viewed as a human right and privacy as a public good, how do we draw lines between selves and others in data environments where we cannot see what (or whom) we expose, and how (for public and private are not clear binaries)?*

§ *How are the pressing issues of the current age bigger and more complex than earlier questions of artisanship versus mass production?*

§ *Are we now tasked with moving towards a post-human algorithm, one that is free of the biases and prejudices (conscious or unconscious) that currently delimit human drives and human(e) choices?*

§ *Finally, with all of its jargon, block boxes and immateriality, how can we look critically at how we talk about digital technology? What lessons can we learn from this exercise?*

The answers to these questions are beyond the scope of this book, but they do illustrate the range of issues that can be opened up to new approaches through a more fundamental incorporation of humanistic and cultural perspectives into the development and critique of big data and indeed software-driven practices, and how necessary such approaches are. A few things we can conclude are, however, that:

- recommender systems based on highly effective algorithms preform individual aesthetic choices and decisions, which can be understood as a massive intervention into consumption habits with yet unknown consequences, leading to their normalization in culture
- the digitization of cultural commons secures the status of the Big Tech corporations and serves the end of predictive analytics based on the 'behavioral surplus' exploited by companies such as Google Books, Amazon Kindle, and Netflix. This is an exploitation of cultural heritage for the profit of private companies and can be termed a 'tragedy of the commons'.[2]
- Big Tech companies have begun to establish content and assume the

role of producers and distributors of cultural products, a development that threatens to displace human cultural production (which, it has been pointed out, serves social functions as processes first, and economic ones as products, second[3]). This trend towards algorithmic cultural production is a form of cultural imperialism or colonialism on the part of the big technology companies.

- the analysis of user behaviour allows the monopolization of knowledge creation processes by private corporations (Amazon, Google Books), which in turn supports a de-differentiation of knowledge production and its uncoupling from the customary social embedding into society.

- what was once the manageable realm of 'discourse' has now become a strange, detached area of information/disinformation/fake news/alternative facts; we have lost our sense of the social dimension of information processing in a world which seemingly has become reigned by algorithms which are not understood by anybody. After all, if the organization responsible for creating a system can't clearly define what they mean when they speak of our data's place in it, how are we supposed to understand any risks we take?

What this book can also do is to provide the framework by which to deliver this more holistic approach, enabling a methodology for the kinds of further studies indicated above. To do this, we need to get beyond viewing culture and datafication as either one and the same or as neutrally disconnected, but perhaps instead as manifestations of different values, hierarchies and beliefs – that is, different cultures.

Is software production also a culture?

These are broad and important considerations, and probably not the ones at the front of your mind as you download a new app or click to agree to its terms of service. Such questions are not individual, so much as cultural, and the problems they raise are only visible at the level where our collectives inform our actions and identities. As such, if you have ever travelled abroad, leaving your home country to experience the language, norms, practices and beliefs of another culture, you may have already experienced the best-possible analog for the state of excitement and expansion of your understanding of the world, but also alienation and tension, that these kinds of technologies place us in. Big data, for all the benefits it brings, has also given rise to tensions and perversions not only of things we think we know, but who we think we are, disrupting practices so intrinsic to individual and social relationships and so sublimated in cultural practices that we can sense, but not necessarily verbalize the change. To address challenges that are hard to perceive, because of our limitations, position, biases or lack of understanding, we need tools to enhance our 'vision': but such instruments, be they microscopes or clean rooms, need to be closely adapted to the precise object of study and the effect it has. This will be no simple achievement. Even the 'digital natives' of the 'Google generation' are not immune to this effect: as one journalist wrote, 'as a typical millennial constantly glued to my phone, my virtual life has fully merged with my real life. There is no difference any more. Tinder is how I meet people, so this is my reality. It is a reality that is constantly being shaped by others – but good luck trying to find out how.'[4]

Part of the insidious and troubling nature of this effect is the manner in which technology has encroached upon our free will in ways that we often cannot even see. We can rebel against censorship when we note something is missing, but how do we seek out perspectives we do not even know we are being denied? Technologies of a certain sort, those that gate not our interaction with the world of objects, but with the inner world of our interpretation and understanding, of the social and the cultural, have always had this effect, to a certain extent. Indeed, it was Plato who gave us the first argument concerning how a new knowledge technology (in Plato's case, writing) gave rise to concerns about the impact it would have on 'memory and wit'. And if writing was the first such case, it was by no means the last: technologies as diverse as the printing press, open library shelves and television have all been heralded as agents to degrade our existing capacities.

Big data and AI, its processing-facing counterpart in the ecosystem of technology assemblages that are growing so exponentially at the moment, can be differentiated from their many predecessors in a number of ways, however. The opacity of these technologies is one reason for this. Big data is big precisely because it is not human-readable; deep fakes are a threat because they are so true to life. Big data and AI lurk silently behind many of our most comfortable spaces, be that the public square where facial recognition is applied to the data streams from its security cameras, the app through which we get to know our future partner or the advertisement targeting serving us credible-looking fake news via our personal social media feeds.

More concerning still, however, is the question of power discussed in Chapter 7, concerns that lurk but one layer further below these algorithms using our personal data to target us. In some cases, this power may indeed be in the hands of a foreign government: the EU High Level Expert Group on fake news and online disinformation[5] recognizes the role of foreign governments in instigating disinformation without naming any particular names, while the rise in cyberterrorism activities by Russia in particular has been highlighted in security committee reports of the US and UK governments.[6] Equally, however, the underlying power may be that of a skilled individual rather than an institutional programme, motivated perhaps by economic need (as in the case of the clickbait mills that arose in the former Yugoslavia in the 2010s[7]), youthful mischief (as in recent hacking of the Twitter accounts of prominent individuals) or a vigilante streak (as in the case of the Anonymous hacktivist collective). But most often, the motivations behind the algorithmic manipulation of social behaviour is not so much a failure of the social and technical systems, but a success, as the greatest power behind the big data systems that control us is of course the companies that in turn control them. In the year 2000, the Fortune 500 list of America's largest companies included only one technology company: IBM. The rest of the list was populated with the usual mix of manufacturing (Ford, Boeing), services (Citigroup, AT&T) and retail (Walmart).[8] Although the manner in which you define 'largest' here matters, by 2020, international rankings – in terms of market capitalization at least – tell a very different story, with only three of the top ten companies <u>not</u> being the high-tech giants, and with Chinese entries like Tencent and Alibaba gaining ground quickly on Microsoft, Apple, Alphabet, Facebook and Amazon.[9]

These companies, valued in the billions, if not trillions, of dollars, have a scale and economic power that eclipses that of many countries. So, if they have a similar scale to countries, do they also have their own culture? If we define culture as the 'knowledge, beliefs, expectations, values, practices, and material objects by means of which we craft meaningful experiences for ourselves and with each other',[10] the answer may seem to be yes. While one might be tempted to view many of these at least as promoters of a very American form of economic and cultural corporate imperialism, there are enough distinct properties common to these subcultures that one can perhaps also speak of a culture of software production, manifested in a view of the world and a sense of place in it that is promoted by and within these collectives, disciplines and organizations. To understand this, we can draw not only on theories of how national cultures manifest in organizational contexts, but also on the many accounts that have been written about the prevailing norms, hierarchies, biases, beliefs, habits of speech, narratives of origin and identity and tolerances within interpersonal interaction, in particular as pertains to issues such as moral and ethical boundaries, perceptions of privacy and so on that have been observed and documented within software companies.

The foundational work regarding cultural approaches to workplace identities and interactions of Geert Hofstede maps in very intriguing ways on to the questions of the work-based habits and cultures of software developers, in spite of the different frame of reference underlying his conclusions (the impact of national cultures on multicultural workplaces and business interactions).[11] Although not all of Hofstede's dimensions map equally precisely on to what can be observed in software development teams, and although one does not want to risk falling back on stereotypes, reflecting on them in this context provides an interesting window for beginning to view software development as a work context with distinct cultural overtones. In particular, the following discussion focuses on five of Hofstede's parameters, in an attempt to at least get a bearing on the centre of gravity for the values and norms underpinning software production.

An obvious place to start is with the dynamic of MASCULINITY VERSUS FEMININITY. This is relevant in spite of the fact that the early workforce of the tech industry, if one can even apply that term to the ecosystem of the 1940s and 1950s around the large main frame systems such as the ENIAC, was strongly feminized. This is clearly not the case today, as studies like Hardey's[12] make all too clear. At that time, coding was viewed as manual labour, 'low on the intellectual and professional status hierarchy'.[13] As the centrality and complexity of the coding process became recognized, however, these tasks were more and more taken over by men. Hand in hand with this shift also came the increasing association of the attributes of a good coder with traditional values of masculinity: an early attempt to develop a psychological profile of programmers concluded that as a group they were avid problem solvers, liked to learn new things and didn't like people.[14] Though one does not want to take gender differences too far towards essentialism, one can see how coding became defined as a space away from the emotional labour so often associated with women in Western societies, 'a refuge from the unpredictability of humans, from their greyscale emotions and needs'.[15] Expanded from a psychological profile to a cultural one, the presence of gender biases in data, code and software products but also a certain engrained tension, if not outright hostility, towards end users of software systems and products can be seen as manifestations of two distinct sets of prevailing attitudes about the world coming into unresolved conflict.

Another interesting point of reflection within Hofstede's taxonomy of national traits is that of LONG or SHORT TERM ORIENTATION. It is perhaps not surprising that software development teams and indeed companies may have an inherent and engrained bias towards the short term. With technology changing so fast, historical or long-term perspectives are inevitably absent in coding circles in particular, as new standards and platforms can arise very quickly to displace existing expertise. In this respect, software engineers may be productively compared to civil, mechanical and other engineers, less than half of whom remain active in development roles for more than a decade past their initial entry into the field.[16] The founding motto of Facebook, 'Move fast and break things', speaks very much to this prevailing attitude in a sector in which the workforce in all of the top tech companies has a median age under forty, with a handful of the leaders in the data revolution, such as Facebook and Google, having a median age below thirty.[17] This leads to what one critic has called 'a world flush with cash and devoid of experience'.[18] And this is surely the point of Facebook having a huge campus providing (controlling) leisure activities, arts, favouring particular aesthetics – demonstrating the culture of the Republic of Facebook, but also celebrating the transformation of technology companies from the conservative dark suit uniform of IBM to the playground-like atmosphere favoured by the successor generation.

The criteria around POWER DISTANCE and INDIVIDUALISM VERSUS COLLECTIVISM are reflected in the manner in which hierarchies and in groups are formed in software development teams. The same culture that has given us the hostility towards users mentioned above has also given us the open-source movement; the same ecosystem that spawned Facebook's 'move fast' motto gave us Google's founding motto of 'don't be evil' (though how much this still resonates with the values and decisions of the company is an open question). Indeed, the lack of diversity in these circles clashes with the industry view of itself as principled, open and meritocratic. The field can appear this way because self-taught amateurs work alongside people with PhDs and because of a certain hacker ethic that brought ' ... a shift in who became a coder and why. For the first time, programmers were emerging in living rooms, as teenagers, propelled by the culture of making, acquiring, and sharing software.'[19] The curiosity, problem orientation and perhaps youthful idealism of the founding generation of software company CEOs have not scaled well as the companies intended to embody these values have acquired trappings that instead befit their size and economic power. Perhaps as a result, coders seem to maintain a stronger loyalty to their tribe, rather than to any particular company or employer.[20]

UNCERTAINTY AVOIDANCE also seems rather baked into the practice of coding, which is highly unforgiving of irregularities or uncertainties. Jeff

Atwood, the founder of programmer's Q&A resource, Stack Overflow, captured this aspect in a reflection on how the interactions on his site represented the best and worst of coder behaviour, with the computer itself as a toxic, abusive colleague: 'The reason a programmer is pedantic is because they work with the ultimate pedant. All this libertarianism, all this "meritocracy", it comes from the computer. I don't think it's actually healthy for people to have that mind-set. It's an occupational hazard. Not everyone is like this. But on average it's correct.'[21] This aspect of software culture became rather a leitmotiv for the KPLEX project, in fact, as so many of the conflicts we observed came down to a desire to preserve the 'hidden treasures' of complexity and the traces of uncertainty in systems with very little tolerance for this.[22]

Finally, Hofstede's categories differentiate between INDULGENCE versus RESTRAINT. This dynamic, so resonant of the preceding discussion of Rousseau's critique of the Enlightenment, may again be visible in the stereotype of the corporate office of the software age (Google, Apple) rather than the hardware age (IBM). Interestingly, however, while this indulgence seems to apply to the trappings of the Fortune 500 lifestyle, it certainly does not reflect the rigour of coding itself, of the methodologies for managing the work processes of software development (such as Agile), or indeed the tendency noted above to put the requirements of the system ahead of those of the user.

Cross-cultural competencies for a Digital Age

This tacit cultural subtext that informs the behaviour of software companies and development teams has wide-ranging effects on the world that now relies on the services they provide, and the flows of how big data is collected and used are a flashpoint where miscommunication, unconscious biases and an underestimation of cultural differences can lead to disasters. At its more benign frontier, the technocratic drive for efficiency suffuses and disrupts our lives, with the fundamental value of optimization and scale being 'what has led to many collisions between software firms and life'.[23] The vulnerability of our attentional spheres[24] is exploited by the ubiquity of notifications and filters designed (in theory at least) to ensure we have the information we need when we need it, but in reality this undermines self-determination in where we place our focus and when, a capacity named as 'intellectual autonomy' by one of the authors of this book.[25] But this perception of humans as essentially incapable can also lead to abuses, in which greater trust is placed in the efficiency of a black box and model behind a data and algorithm-driven system than in social responsibility of our fellow human beings. The perceived superior efficiency and neutrality of machines in the face of ethical and challenging decisions have led to a range of cases in which delegation of traditionally human decisions has led to abuses of not just social contracts but human rights. In particular the deployment of the Compas system,[26] in which the opaque projections of past inequalities were used to determine the future confinement or freedom of individuals, demonstrates how the tension between human social responsibility and their fallibility can become dangerously entangled with efficiency.

Many of the systems are of course open to abusive deployments as well, as can be seen in the case of the Cambridge Analytica role in swaying public opinion and/or manipulating (via suppression or stimulation) of voting via social media in the 2016 US election and UK referendum on leaving the EU. The fact that the mechanism for gathering the data to build the system behind this masqueraded as academic research makes this abuse all the more galling. But even if such systems can be regulated, used properly and held to high ethical standards, the centrality of the perception that machine efficiency trumps the slow and underinformed decision-making processes of the human being can still lead to perverse and disconcerting outcomes, such as the evidence we see that humans, from pilots to translators, relying on artificial intelligence in their professional lives can actually lose competency over time.[27] If ethical decision making, scientific discovery and the development of informed citizens also come to be seen as equally inefficient processes, one may fear where the biases and blinders of technology will leave us.

Our fear of inefficiency leaves us open the abuses of our focus in the so-called 'attention economy'. An infamous holy writ of early technology, Nir Eyal's *Hooked*, made much of the many ways that human psychological weaknesses could be exploited to meet some of the technological success metrics of 'stickiness' and repeat visits.[28] This approach positions behavioural engineering as a direct inlet port for technology into culture, a value also confirmed by former Google senior manager (now founder of the Centre for Humane Technology and their centrepiece initiative 'Time Well Spent') Tristan Harris: 'the job of these companies is to hook people, and they do that by hijacking our psychological vulnerabilities'.[29]

Perhaps an even better example of precisely how disciplinary and corporate cultures can lead to assumptions and ultimately to disasters on a grand scale, in particular where the drivers of these disasters may be hidden within the sea of big data behind a proprietary system, is that of Facebook's entry into Myanmar.

In this case, the collision of data-centric floods of misinformation, such as were discussed in Chapter 2 of this book, power dynamics and a disregard for a receiving culture are very clearly illustrated. In essence, the situation in Myanmar was a sort of 'perfect storm', where underlying tensions between social groups and a perfectly timed change in telecoms regulation left the country vulnerable to a rise in unrest. Facebook took advantage of this latter shift, establishing itself via a loss-leading pricing for data access, as the dominant face of the internet in the country. It then however ignored warnings that their platform was being used to share and broadcast hate speech. According to a Reuters news report[30] as of 2014, they reportedly had only one (Dublin-based) content reviewer who spoke Burmese on staff: by 2015 this number had risen only to four, for a pool of 7.3 million active users. And, even as late as 2018, the company had no actual staff in Myanmar, with only outsourced contractors offshore to oversee the interactions they were facilitating. It is perhaps easy to point a finger at Facebook as a single company, but the evidence shows this gaping hole in perception to be more widespread than only theirs: former Google CEO Eric Schmidt commented in 2009 that studying global usage patterns of his company's search engine convinced him that 'people are the same everywhere', and that 'people still care about Britney Spears in these other countries'.[31]

Facebook not only underestimated the cultural challenges in Myanmar, of language but also of social cohesion, they also overestimated the power of their machine translation systems to be able to accurately flag dangerous content, and provide a technical fix to a cultural problem. But of course, machine translation has traditionally only been as good as the big data available to train the software, which means that results seen functioning well between languages like English, French and German can raise highly misleading expectations regarding languages like Burmese (or indeed Icelandic, as was discussed in Chapter 7). The arrogance associated with this particular corporate asset can also be seen in Mark Zuckerberg's own post from May 2017, in which he announced the publication of the Facebook translation software code. The post concluded with the self-congratulatory, and highly misguided, claims:

> Throughout human history, language has been a barrier to communication. It's amazing we get to live in a time when technology can change that. Understanding someone's language brings you closer to them, and I'm looking forward to making universal translation a reality.[32]

Claiming that language is a barrier to communication utterly perverts the role that this subtle and varied human achievement has played throughout the history of our species. It also greatly overestimates the capacity of machine translation to capture the essence of communication: indeed, the best neural network-driven translations can often hide more than they share by producing very plausible natural language outputs, which, however, utterly misrepresent the sentiments of the original utterance. In the case of Myanmar, however, the communication seemed to have been all too clear, while the engrained hubris of Facebook and its engineers in the tools they had proven valid according to their own cultural norms, were unable to see this, even as it unfolded in real time on their own servers and the streets of Mandalay. And, while Myanmar may be the most extreme example of this, it is far from exceptional: as when it comes to product design, culture matters (though perhaps it is very often only addressed in a very simplistic manner). Speaking of an example of a development team considering what protections might be incorporated into an early version of Twitter, Clive Thompson writes:

> The team of young guys who made it were, demographically, far less likely to have experienced online abuse. They didn't prioritize it early on as an inevitable, looming problem they would need to address. On the contrary, one staff member dubbed their company "the free-speech wing of the free-speech party." They designed few safeguards against harassment, and years later, trolls and white supremacists discovered that Twitter was a fabulous way to harass targets.[33]

The manner in which shared identities and groupthink at odds with common values and norms seem to pervade the development of software is reminiscent of Benedict Anderson's seminal work on the idea of imaginary communities, group-based labels representing masses of shared cultural capital, utterly intangible, and yet inspiring of loyalty even unto death. Anjuan Simmon's theory that software companies have not only begun to act like countries, but, indeed like the colonial powers of old, is a both compelling and frightening extension of this: 'Technology companies today are increasingly colonial in their actions. This can be seen in the veneer of sovereignty they seek to cultivate, how they work across borders, their use of dominant culture as a weapon, and the clear belief that "superior" technology is a suitable excuse for lawlessness, exploitation and even violence.'[34]

But where do these identities arise from? As described above, a certain amount of the acculturation of software engineers may come from personal predilections, preferences that may be linked to psychology or early experiences of reward and competence. But if values and habits can be identified in what is essentially a culture of immigrants (there may be habits of mind and thought that attract people to coding, but one would assume that few people are born into such an identity), then we may also usefully look at how young software developers are trained to absorb the values of their tribe, the incentives and penalties that exist, and indeed where the possible tops of the hierarchies may be found (e.g. in training and degree programmes), as these could be entry points for investigation or even intervention that might bring data-driven approaches to knowledge back in line with identities and cultural affordances (or at least buffer their effect to a speed at which norms can assimilate them).

We have explored examples of things that have happened, but what about things that might or could happen? In particular, the symbiotic relationship between big data and AI raise the stakes for what new risks might arise in the future. Making sense of the masses of individually captured records of actions and phenomena, from the exact temperature at a certain point on the globe at a certain moment, to the search terms entered in every Google search you have ever made, requires the patience, precision and speed of a machine applying an algorithmic model to make sense of. And, sometimes, the software parsing this data is not merely looking for patterns defined by its designer, but is using the data it has been given to 'learn' from patterns and correlations that may exist in it, but which even the software developer may not have recognized. It is here that we enter the realm of artificial intelligence and can see how it builds upon the potential of the big data corpora by learning and extracting patterns from it. The problem is, however, that at a certain point, even the engineer who designed the system may not understand how the conclusions were derived from the training data. It is from this phenomenon that we can find data biases leading to the development of systems that identify people of colour as gorillas, and even systems that have been found to 'cheat' (e.g. by using embedded metadata about an image rather than the visual content itself as a way to identify the object of a photograph).[35] So problematic have some of these data sources been found to be when big data is used to train AI that in one case MIT had to permanently decommission the popular Tiny Images dataset and urge users to delete off-line copies they might be using, after the data was found to regularly produce racist and sexist labelling of the images.[36]

As technology becomes more complex, the threats it poses escalate to become overarching, targeting democracy, security, the individual right to self-determination and collective claims on maintaining cultural practices undisturbed by the intrusion of companies with a distinct set of practices that may or may not accurately reflect those of their users. It is here where a recognition of the cultural dimension of the conflict playing out can be particularly useful, as the long tradition of reflection and practice regarding the easing of intercultural tensions and misunderstandings can be applied to perhaps provide new foundations for developing personal and regulatory 'green lights and red lines' for overseeing the development of software platforms and products that collect and reuse our data.

Intercultural competence has cognitive, affective and behavioural dimensions. Its toolkit includes *knowledge* about other cultures, which enables a refined understanding of the nature of culture and a wariness of oversimplification. In addition, it fosters the development of personality traits such as empathy, openness and flexibility which are enablers of intercultural dialogue. Finally, it fosters an understanding of the subtlety of communication and a rigour towards the potential for miscommunication and misunderstanding, which one must assume is present in such encounters with inherent difference. It ensures that our hermeneutic powers, the cornerstone of humanistic investigation, do not get lulled into trusting false heuristics, mindful of Friedrich Schleiermacher's advice that 'misunderstanding occurs as a matter of course, and understanding must therefore be willed and sought at every point'.[37]

Applying strategies developed to navigate intercultural interactions can provide a number of concrete supports to individual and collective responses to new and developing software platforms and tools, in particular ones that are facilitated by the gathering and use of big data. For example, the discussion of how unconscious biases have come to shape the products of big data is now well known and discussed in its cultural dimensions throughout this book. We can speak of these biases in a number of ways, such as the effects they have, the human rights they may infringe upon and the contributing factors that may cause them to be expressed in software, but none of these approaches has yet developed into a basis for strategies to both understand and counteract their incursion. It is instructive therefore to look at this problem in the light of some of the work on impediments to intercultural interaction, such as the framework developed by Brislin in the 1980s,[38] which included three parameters: prejudice, stereotypes and ethnocentrism. Although a more comprehensive mapping of these factors to the interaction between software creators and users will require more extensive study, evidence of all of these factors has already been seen above: prejudice (defined as a 'dislike based on a wrong and inflexible generalization') seems to well encompass the tensions between the 'coder' and the user, and ethnocentrism (defined as the 'tendency to view one's own culture as the only appropriate way of life') is also hugely resonant with the tensions reflected in many of the accounts of conflicts between software developers and their management.

Perhaps most interesting of Brislin's three parameters, however, is that of stereotypes, which he defines as 'an exaggerated assumption about a certain category of people'. One can see this aspect realized perhaps most forcefully in the popular technology design tool known as a 'persona'. These snapshot biographies of potential users may have come into fashion as a way to 'help you step out of yourself'[39] as a technology designer, but the narrowing of user profiles down to the details of one particular (fictional) person's likes and dislikes, to the extent of including quotes in their imagined 'voice', largely promotes a reference to simplified stereotypes rather than the complexity of human experience. As an extension of the thinking of software culture, personas act as a way of promoting the cultural imperialism that forces the users to adapt to tools, rather than the other way around.

Intercultural competencies don't only give us a capacity to perceive and understand software development, they also give us strategies to respond to it differently. For example, Oberg's taxonomy of stages in adjusting to intercultural interaction[40] provides a very useful lens for observing some of the shifts in the relationship between users, their data and technology platforms. The first stage is known as the **Honeymoon Stage:** characterized by fascination and enthusiasm, and friendly but superficial relations between cultures. The many benefits of new technology, innovative uses for it and the habits that will predicate its later expansion are established in this stage. Before we had the Cambridge Analytica scandal, we saw Egypt's 'Facebook Revolution'; and before we saw publicly shared DNA records[41] become a possible bounty for the surveillance assemblages of insurance companies and law enforcement, we saw a groundswell of public interest in what their genetic data could tell them about their health and their family histories. Regardless of whether the potential for abuse is always inherent in them, or emerges only as technologies become widespread and accepted enough for abuses of privacy and attention to emerge, it is clear that at this point in many cases we have segued in our relationship to the second phase of intercultural **Crisis,** in which culture shock arises as a result of differences in languages, values, etc., such as the many documented in this book, which lead to feelings of loss, rejection, frustration, anxiety or anger.

The open question is of course how the ecosystem of interactions between individuals and their data, and the companies and systems that use them, can make the next two shifts, first to **Recovery**, in which the crisis is gradually resolved, as the expatriate starts to learn how to act within the norms of the new language and culture and finally **Adjustment,** in which the expatriate accepts cultural differences and even comes to appreciate them, although there may still be occasional instances of anxiety. We can see progress against these phases in the shift over time in how the conversation around ethics for big data and AI are developing, however. These phases (as documented by Kind)[42] have moved discussions of AI ethics from initially being led by ethicists and philosophers, producing strong and informed responses, but expressed in a language and cultural code very foreign to those building software, to proposals consisting of technical fixes, emerging from the software development community in response to criticism of their output. What is emerging now in the 'third wave' of ethical frameworks to govern large technological systems is an approach with a much more hybrid set of actors, including regulators and the courts, citizen activists, NGOs and independent think tanks.

The work that underpins this book was designed in conversation with this third wave, but also aimed to address some of the gaps between the first and second ones, drawing from a deep understanding of culture to suggest ways in which technology builders and users might productively converge on a set of principles to guide a new generation of software design. To do so effectively, we must, however, be very clear, with ourselves and with our readers, about the biases and values we ourselves bring to this work. Each of us is steeped in both the appreciation of and the professional study of culture and its place in our lives. When we observe how the knowledge technologies we write of are deployed in society, we see them not only through the filter of what they are and do, but also of the creative memory- and identity-forming processes they are silent participants in. We are each personally and professionally committed to the translation between these values and their possible actuation in software.

While it is not clear if software culture has come close to realizing the vision of technologies being developed 'by the people for the people'[43] viewing software development as culture allows us to read the conflicts between culture moving at a human's pace and the much faster machine and corporate drives to datafication, as intercultural relations: after all, software systems and the people who build them do display distinct languages, norms, shared understandings, biases and ethics. This holistic approach will hopefully not only complement strategies to guide responses to developments in the digital society growing out of the social sciences, but also enable a paradigm allowing humanities methods and knowledge to take a leading role in the study of the digital in human cultures and lives.

Notes

1　Zuboff, Shoshana, *The Age of Surveillance Capitalism* (London: Profile Books, 2019).

2　Yakowitz Bambauer, Jane R., 'Tragedy of the Data Commons', *Harvard Journal of Law and Technology*, 25/1 (2011), 1–67.

3　Hertzmann, Aaron. 'Computers Do Not Make Art, People Do', *Communications of the ACM*, 63/5 (May 2020), 45–8.

4　Duportail, Judith, 'I Asked Tinder for My Data. It Sent Me 800 Pages of My Deepest, Darkest Secrets', *The Guardian* (2017), http://www.theguardian.com/technology/2017/sep/26/tinder-personal-data-dating-app-messages-hacked-sold.

5　European Commission, 2018.

6　Intelligence and Security Committee of Parliament, 'Intelligence and Security Committee of Parliament Annual Report 2016–2017' (2017), 123.

7　Subramanian, Samanth, 'Inside the Macedonian Fake-news Complex', *WIRED* (2017), https://www.wired.com/2017/02/veles-macedonia-fake-news/

8　Fortune 500 2000, https://fortune.com/fortune500/2000/.

9　The 100 largest companies in the world by market capitalization in 2020, https://www.statista.com/statistics/263264/top-companies-in-the-world-by-market-capitalization/.

10　McLean, Paul, *Culture in Networks* (Cambridge: Wiley, 2017), 1.

11　Hofstede, Geert, 'Dimensionalizing Cultures: The Hofstede Model in Context', *Online Readings in Psychology and Culture*, 2/1 (1 December 2011).

12　Hardey, Mariann, *The Culture of Women in Tech: An Unsuitable Job for a Woman* (Emerald Publishing, 2019).

13　Ensmenger, Nathan L., *The Computer Boys Take Over Computers, Programmers, and the Politics of Technical Expertise* (Cambridge, MA: MIT Press), 15.

14　Cannon, William M. and Dallis K. Perry, 'A Vocational Interest Scale for Computer Programmers', in *Proceedings of the Fourth SIGCPR Conference on Computer Personnel Research*, SIGCPR '66 (New York: Association for Computing Machinery, 1966), 61–82.

15　Thompson, Clive, *Coders: Who They Are, What They Think and How They Are Changing Our World* (London: Picador, 2019), 77.

16　Frehill, Lisa, 'Satisfaction: Why Do People Give up on Engineering? Surveys of Men and Women Engineers Tell an Unexpected Story', *Mechanical Engineering*, 132/01 (2010), 38–41.

17　Bort, Julie, 'Some Tech Workers over 50 Are Literally Working Themselves to Death – and Other Things We Discovered about Their Careers', *Business Insider,* https://www.businessinsider.com/stressful-lives-of-older-tech-workers-2015-11.

18 Lyons, Dan, *Disrupted: Ludicrous Misadventures in the Tech Start-up Bubble* (London: Atlantic Books, 2017).

19 Thompson, *Coders,* 44.

20 Stevens, Barry, 'Probing the DP Psyche', *Computerworld* (21 July 1980), 26.

21 Quoted in Thompson, *Coders: The Making of a New Tribe and the Remaking of the World*, 68–9.

22 Kouw, Matthijs, Andrea Scharnhorst and Charles Heuvel, 'Exploring Uncertainty. Classifications, Simulations and Models of the World' (2013), 89–125, https://www.researchgate.net/publication/260438168_Exploring_Uncertainty_Classifications_Simulations_and_Models_of_the_World.

23 Thompson, *Coders,* 45.2.

24 Crawford, Matthew B., *The World beyond Your Head: On Becoming an Individual in an Age of Distraction*. Reprint edition. (New York: Farrar, Straus and Giroux, 2016).

25 Horsley, N., 'Intellectual Autonomy after Artificial Intelligence: The Future of Memory Institutions and Historical Research', in *Big Data – A New Medium?* (Abingdon: Routledge, 2020), 130–44.

26 Correctional Offender Management Profiling for Alternative Sanctions (COMPAS) is proprietary software that uses algorithms that are trade secrets to assess the risk of recidivism in criminal defendants and is used by courts in the USA to aid judges in sentencing. It has been shown to discriminate against black people.

27 Cited in Awati, Kailash and Simon Buckingham Shum, 'Big Data Metaphors We Live By' (14 May 2015), https://towardsdatascience.com/big-data-metaphors-we-live-by-98d3fa44ebf8.

28 Eyal, Nir, *Hooked Book – Product Design to Boost Customer Engagement* (Bingley: Portfolio Penguin, 2013).

29 Leslie, Ian, 'The Scientists Who Make Apps Addictive', *The Economist* (20 October 2016), https://www.economist.com/1843/2016/10/20/the-scientists-who-make-apps-addictive.

30 Stecklow, Steve, 'Why Facebook Is Losing the War on Hate Speech in Myanmar', *Reuters* (15 August 2018), https://www.reuters.com/investigates/special-report/myanmar-facebook-hate/.

31 Google, *Eric Schmidt, Princeton Colloquium on Public & Int'l Affairs* (2009), https://www.youtube.com/watch?v=9nXmDxf7D_g.

32 Mark Zuckerberg, (10 May 2017), Facebook update.

33 Thompson, *Coders,* 24.

34 Simmons, Anjuan, 'Technology Colonialism', *Model View Culture* (2015), https://modelviewculture.com/pieces/technology-colonialism.

35 Coldewey, Devin, 'This Clever AI Hid Data from Its Creators to Cheat at Its Appointed Task', *TechCrunch*, (31 December 2018), https://social.techcrunch.com/2018/12/31/this-clever-ai-hid-data-from-its-creators-to-cheat-at-its-appointed-task/.

36 Quach, Katyanna, 'MIT Apologizes, Permanently Pulls Offline Huge Dataset That Taught AI Systems to Use Racist, Misogynistic Slurs', *The Register,* https://www.theregister.com/2020/07/01/mit_dataset_removed/.

37 Kimmerle, Heinz, *Hermeneutics: The Handwritten Manuscripts* (Atlanta: Oxford University Press, 1986).

38 Brislin, R. W., *Cross-cultural Encounters* (New York: Pergamon Press, 1981).

39 Dam, Rikke Friis and Teo Yu Siang, 'Personas – A Simple Introduction', *The Interaction Design Foundation* (2020), https://www.interaction-design.org/literature/article/personas-why-and-how-you-should-use-them.

40 Oberg Kalervo, 'Cultural Shock: Adjustment to New Cultural Environments', *Practical Anthropology,* 7/4 (1960), 177–82. doi:10.1177/009182966000700405.

41 A concern most recently aired when it was announced that leading private DNA testing company 23andMe was planning to go public: https://www.theguardian.com/technology/2021/feb/09/23andme-dna-privacy-richard-branson-genetics.

42 Kind, Carly, 'The Term "Ethical AI" Is Finally Starting to Mean Something' *VentureBeat* (23 August 2020), https://venturebeat.com/2020/08/23/the-term-ethical-ai-is-finally-starting-to-mean-something/.

43 Kalluri, Pratyusha, 'Don't Ask If Artificial Intelligence Is Good or Fair, Ask How It Shifts Power', *Nature*, 583/7815 (7 July 2020), 169.

Index